REVOLUTIONARY
TERRORISM

REVOLUTIONARY TERRORISM

The FLN in Algeria, 1954–1962

Martha Crenshaw Hutchinson

HOOVER INSTITUTION PRESS

Stanford University • Stanford, California

Material from "The Concept of Revolutionary Terrorism" was previously published in *Journal of Conflict Resolution*. It is here reprinted (pp. 18–39) by permission of the publisher, Sage Publications, Inc.

Hoover Institution Publication 196

International Standard Book Number: 0–8179–6961–6
Library of Congress Catalog Card Number: 78–59130
Printed in the United States of America

To Bill

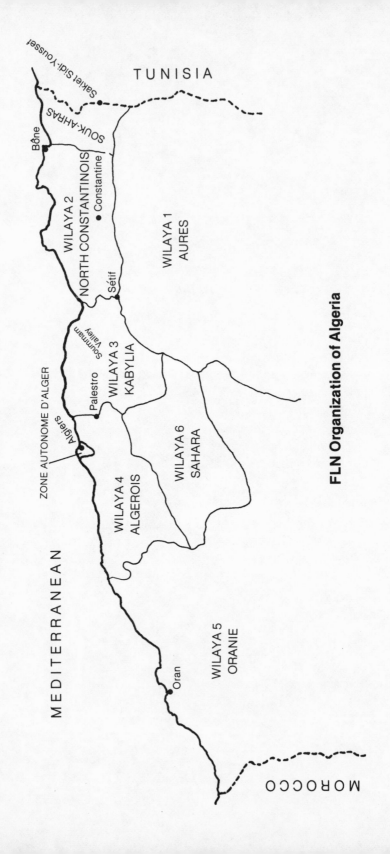

FLN Organization of Algeria

Contents

Acknowledgments

Edward A. Kolodziej has been a source of inspiration and good advice since my graduate student days, when I first became intrigued with the problem of terrorism. He, along with Inis L. Claude, Jr., advised on the dissertation that was the origin of this book. I want to thank Raymond Aron, Edward Behr, Roger Trinquier, Germaine Tillion, and Eric Westphal for discussing the project with me. The University of Virginia awarded a fellowship for a year's research in Paris; the *Fondation National des Sciences Politiques* allowed me to use their excellent library and press-clipping files; the *Université de Poitiers* offered me the position of *lectrice*, which enabled me to write the first draft of this manuscript; and Wesleyan University has provided support for subsequent rewritings. Louise Fosa and Rhonda Kissinger helped greatly with the typing. My gratitude also extends to J. Bowyer Bell, for his faith in this enterprise, and to Peter Kilby, for his encouragement and help. My husband, however, has had to tolerate more terrorism than anyone else, so it is to him that this book is dedicated. I am tempted to blame its faults on him as well, but honesty compels me to take them on myself.

Introduction

Terrorism as a strategy of opposition to an established political order is an issue that provokes lively and intense debate, but it proves an intractable subject for scholarly inquiry. The immediacy of the practical problem and the emotions it arouses are not conducive to objective analysis. The complicated nature of the phenomenon, which cuts across conventional academic fields and interests government officials as much as scholars, and the abundance of historical examples prevent easy investigation or explanation. There is scarcely any agreement on a definition of terrorism, much less a general theory. Impassioned discussion has not brought us much closer to understanding the attractiveness of terrorism as a revolutionary strategy or why and how it is effective in causing political change. What are the reasons for such extraordinary and risky violence? Is terrorism rational, pathological, or criminal? What are the consequences of its use? What policies should and do governments adopt in response to this challenge?

Answers to these questions are obscured by the controversy surrounding the study of contemporary terrorism. Some people feel compelled to make explicit or implicit moral judgements—to choose sides for or against terrorism. Terrorism is often any violence perpetrated by those with whom one disagrees. Other analysts are tempted to seek comprehensiveness by adopting approaches that claim to encompass all historical instances of terrorism; consequently they propose vague and unfounded generalities about the terrorist "personality" or the apocalyptic consequences of spreading violence.

This study is an analysis of a single case of terrorism, that of the Front de Libération Nationale (FLN) during the Algerian war, 1954–1962. Focusing on this example facilitates the intensive evaluation and thorough understanding that are often lost in more general studies, and choosing an example from the recent past rather than the present provides relevance to contemporary events, the requisite historical distance for objectivity, and the opportunity to assess a final outcome. I also hope that this approach to the analysis of terrorism—especially breaking it down into a number of conceptual categories—will provide a sound basis for further study.

Terrorism is hardly a novel method of political opposition. To give an idea of the continuity of the phenomenon, I will briefly place the Algerian case in historical perspective.[1]

The first deliberate and systematic use of terrorist violence in the service of a secular political ideology was the "Terror" of the French Revolution. The term "terrorism" owes its origin to that series of events. The French Revolution is an example of revolutionary terrorism that is perpetrated by an elite in power against its citizens, but the policy of using violence to undermine potential resistance and directing it against classes of people rather than specific individuals foreshadows the terrorism of certain post–World War II national liberation movements. It is a more intimate precursor of the totalitarian terror of Hitler and of Stalin. Regime terrorism, however, is not the concern of this study.

The Russian revolutionaries, who were active from the last quarter of the nineteenth century on, were the originators of the strategy of terrorism as a political assault against an indigenous autocracy. For the most part an elite drawn from the intelligentsia, the Russian terrorists formed conspiracies to assassinate prominent officials of the regime. The first wave of symbolic assassinations culminated in the bomb that killed Alexander II in 1881. His death failed to bring about the political reforms that the People's Will organization sought; instead it provoked a repression from which emerged a new generation of terrorists committed to revolution—the Combat Organization of the Socialist-Revolutionary party, which was active from 1901 until the eve of World War I. The terrorism of both groups was characterized by discrimination in the selection of victims, who were high government officials or police spies.

The use of terrorism to win national independence from a foreign power was also inaugurated before the turn of the century. The Internal Macedonian Revolutionary Organization (IMRO) was active from the 1890s to the late 1920s in an unsuccessful attempt to win independence from the Ottoman Empire and later from the Bulgarian state. The Irish were more successful in their struggle for autonomy from the British. The Easter Rising of 1916, which was unsuccessful as a catalyst to a mass revolt, marked a turn toward the use of terrorism against the British security apparatus in Ireland and against Irish "informers." (The Land League had already initiated agrarian terrorism against landlords.) The Irish Republican Army (IRA) under Michael Collins aimed for the middle levels of military and police administration, particularly the intelligence branches, rather than the political officials at the top as the Russian revolutionaries had done. Although the extreme nationalists failed to win the goal of total Irish independence from Britain, their terrorism, by putting pressure on the British government, benefited the moderates who accepted the establishment of the Irish Free State.

The cause for which terrorism was principally employed in the post-war era was nationalism in various forms. In the Palestine Mandate, the Irgun Zvai Leumi and Lehi (Stern Gang) fought the British in the name of Zionism. In Malaya and in Vietnam, the insurgents were Communist-led. On Cyprus, the EOKA, reflecting Greek more than Cypriot nationalism, was committed to union with Greece, not to Cypriot independence. The nationalism of the Kenyan Mau Mau was based on tribal loyalties as much as on secular political aspirations. In North Africa, the power of Islam and the Arab identity buttressed national liberation movements.

Some of these campaigns of terrorism occurred in conjunction with full-scale anti-imperialist insurrections; others were limited revolts. In Kenya, Malaya, Algeria, and Vietnam, terrorism was part of a struggle for control of the indigenous population, combined with extensive rural or jungle guerrilla warfare. Civilians from potential constituencies as well as from the enemy community were frequently victims of terrorism. In Malaya, the situation was complicated by the fact that the insurgents were recruited mainly from the Chinese minority, not the Malay majority who opposed their ambitions. In Palestine and in Cyprus, the terrorists were a narrowly based elite who did not try to create a clandestine mass organization. Their terrorism was aimed primarily at the structure of British authority (although the EOKA also targeted civilian Cypriot "traitors").

The EOKA, the Kenyan Mau Mau, and the Malayan communists failed to achieve their immediate aims, although the British eventually granted independence to all three states. The Zionist terrorists were more successful with their tactics aimed at shaming the British into departure. In Vietnam and in Algeria, the national liberation fronts emerged victorious after years of struggle, in which terrorism played an important part.

Algeria was a classic case of revolutionary nationalist terrorism against a colonial power. It involved extensive communal strife between Muslims and Europeans, including the formation of a European terrorist movement, the Organisation de l'Armée Secrète (OAS), in reaction to the FLN. The FLN employed a broad range of terrorist tactics in combination with mass organization, propaganda, guerrilla warfare, and diplomacy. Terrorism in Algeria took on a distinctly international cast. Both the IMRO and IRA (and even the Fenians in the nineteenth century) had employed violence in the capitals of the foreign powers, and the FLN mounted a campaign of terrorism in metropolitan France in 1958. The FLN also deliberately sought international publicity, as the Zionists had done. The subsequent reputation of FLN terrorism—its value as a model for future national liberation organizations—is also worth mentioning. The film *The Battle of Algiers,* a picturesque portrayal of courageous freedom fighters pitted against blundering colonial soldiers, has since popularized the image of revolutionary terrorism. Frantz Fanon, the ideologue of the Algerian revolution, has attained the status of prophet to many would-be revolutionaries. Whether or not the FLN example was an appropriate inspiration for subsequent terrorists, it has attained an important position in the history of revolution.

Three significant developments mark the postcolonial wave of terrorism of the late 1960s and 1970s. First, the transnational aspect of this new terrorism continues the trend toward the internationalization of revolutionary conflict initiated by earlier radical groups such as the IRA, the Irgun, and the FLN. Violence now crosses national frontiers with ease, and terrorism is a conscious and sometimes exclusive search for global attention and publicity.[2] The search for international recognition and the use of violence in the colonial metropolis are not new tactics; the practice of attacking nationals of states outside the immediate scope of the conflict may also have originated with the Stern Group's assassination of United Nations mediator Count Folke Bernadotte in 1948. However, the Palestinian resistance organizations have escalated the politics of violent confrontation with their random targeting of civilians, usually airline passengers, who have no official connection with their struggle.

A second feature of modern terrorism is the use of violence as a tool for bargaining with governments. The seizure of hostages to compel a government to make specific concessions originated in Latin America. The first demands for the release of political prisoners soon escalated to huge monetary ransoms. Bargaining also took on a transnational character with the kidnapping of foreign diplomats. The seizure of large numbers of hostages by hijacking aircraft was initiated by the Palestinian resistance. These developments have no precedent in the Algerian case; the FLN occasionally practiced kidnapping, but not for ransom.

The third modern development may not be as novel as the other two factors. This is the prevalence of terrorism against the developed capitalist states of the West. This violence has two sources, neither of them revolutionary. On the one hand, regional or ethnic separatist movements have used terrorism in attempts to dismember established states. The Basque ETA, the Front de Libération du Quebec, and, to a lesser extent, the Provisional IRA in Ulster are examples of this category. On the other hand, groups such as the Rote Armee Fraktion or Baader-Meinhof group in West Germany, the Japanese Red Army, the Symbionese Liberation Army and the Weathermen in the United States, as well as several Italian groups can perhaps best be classified as neoanarchist. Their aim is the destruction of order but they have no clearly formulated conception of a new political and social framework to replace the old. Furthermore, their perception of corruption and oppression is not shared by the societies in which they operate. Their potential for acquiring popular support is limited. Anarchist violence against the bourgeoisie is not new. Modern terrorists follow in the footsteps of the nineteenth-century anarchists who, practicing the "propaganda of the deed," alarmed the governments of Britain, France, Spain, Italy, and the United States.

Since no clear definition of the concept of terrorism has emerged from the study of these many instances, I begin this analysis with a definition of revolutionary terrorism and an explanation of its use as a strategy of political violence. I then apply this definition to the complicated series of events that comprised the Algerian war to distinguish terrorism from the other forms of violence that were used. It should become evident that revolutionary terrorism includes several different categories of actions, which can be classified according to their political functions in the revolution. Analyzing acts of terrorism in terms of the intentions of the revolutionary leaders, the social groups the acts were meant to affect, the psychological and political reactions they were meant to inspire, and the methods of violence used, makes it possible to judge the sometimes paradoxical consequences of these phenomena. To evaluate the effectiveness of terrorism without understanding the purposes of the terrorists is impossible. For example, terrorism is often thought to be self-defeating because it arouses hostility, but if the terrorists want attention at any cost rather than approval, then opprobrium is a successful result from their perspective. Although the Algerian people constituted the vast majority of the victims of FLN terrorism, the FLN not only coerced their obedience but attracted genuine popular allegiance. The French policy toward terrorism was partially responsible for the FLN's successes in acquiring popular support, and valuable lessons can be learned from the mistakes of the French. I conclude with some general propositions about the causes, processes, and effectiveness of revolutionary terrorism.

My major contention, that the terrorism of the FLN was the result of deliberate political calculations, does not constitute a moral judgment on the choice of terrorism as a means to an end. The interpretation of terrorism as an activity to be understood in terms of the political and social goals of its users does not imply an ethical judgment about its justifiability. Nor is criticism of the French response to terrorism meant as moral condemnation. Regrettable as this stand may seem to the committed on one side or the other, the problem of the morality of violence is outside the scope of this study.

The FLN
and the Algerian Context

I

FLN terrorism occurred in the context of a nationalist revolution against French rule in Algeria. An examination of this political and social background is essential to understanding the causes and the effectiveness of terrorism. This chapter is an analysis of the conditions leading to revolution, especially the development of Algerian nationalism, the characteristics of the FLN's organization, leadership, and ideology, and an outline of the FLN's general revolutionary strategy from November 1954 to June 1962.

THE CONDITIONS OF REVOLUTION

The methods and goals of French colonialism in Algeria partially explain the desperation of the group of nationalists who began the revolution in 1954. The French conquered Algeria almost accidentally and pursued a policy of colonization in an undirected and aimless fashion from 1830 until 1871, when the last serious indigenous resistance was broken and the territory was at last transferred from military to civilian rule.

The character and interests of the European settlers in Algeria were important determinants of the causes, the strategy, and the consequences of the Algerian revolution. By the turn of the century, the substantial European minority had become native; most of these Europeans had been born in Algeria and felt separate and distinct from their metropolitan compatriots, whom they often regarded with scorn for their "softness." By 1954 there were in Algeria approximately a million French citizens of diverse European origins, mostly Mediterranean, known colloquially as *pieds noirs*. Over three-quarters of them were employed in commerce and industry and lived in Algeria's cities and towns on the coastal plains. More than two-thirds of the rural land-holders were small farmers, but the wealthy *colons* controlled the best lands (85 percent of the European-owned total) and possessed inordinate political influence. Vineyards producing wine exports were the mainstay of the colonial economy, which was heavily dependent on the French market. In contrast, the Muslim population had lost the most fertile lands to Europeans; in 1954 only five hundred Muslims had substantial landholdings.[1]

The history of French colonization in Algeria centers on the concept of "assimilation." To the metropolitan French, this meant bringing the benefits of French civilization and culture to the native Muslim population of Algeria—an expression of the French humanitarian and universalist "mission civilisatrice."[2] To the colons of Algeria, however, assimilation, or its post-1954 version known as "integration," meant the maintenance of Algeria as an integral, inseparable part of France, of their rights as French citizens, and of their domination over the local population.

After 1871 Algeria was governed not in the interest of France or of the Muslim majority, but for the benefit of the European minority. The disastrous impact of the military conquest and of colonial rule on the social, cultural, linguistic, religious, and economic structures of Algeria was completely disregarded. The traditional life of Algeria was literally destroyed and replaced with an alien system from which Algerians were excluded. Lands, especially the most fertile coastal plains, were seized for European cultivation, leaving the Algerian peasants with sparse plots from which only a bare subsistence could be won. Partial famines were followed by serious epidemics of disease among the local populations in 1893, 1897, and 1920. The indigenous elites, both urban and rural, were broken; their functions, especially the administration of justice, were taken over by French officials who relied on docile and cooperative, rather than representative or respected, Muslims. Until 1927, Algerian life was governed by the 1881 Code de l'Indigénat, which allowed civil administrators to retain the exceptional powers held by military officers during the early period of conquest. A special tax was imposed on the Muslim population until 1919. In general, despite social and economic benefits such as improved health care and agricultural development, the French regime in Algeria was one of obstinate and authoritarian paternalism.[3]

After the First World War, the situation slowly began to change. One instigating factor was the rapid population growth of the Algerian people. This created even more rural misery, causing migrations from the countryside to the cities of Algeria and of France. It was among the workers in France that the first stirrings of Algerian nationalism began, and the contacts with French life that urbanization implied contributed to the realization by the Algerians of their inferior position.

In 1926, the energetic and persistent leader Messali Hadj created in France the Etoile Nord-Africaine (ENA), a movement with a proletarian, revolutionary, and nationalistic orientation. The French reacted suspiciously to this development, banning the organization twice and constantly arresting Messali. In 1937, the ENA narrowed its focus from all of the Maghreb to Algeria and became the Parti du Peuple Algérien (PPA), which was itself banned two years later. At the same time, a strong reformist religious movement, determined to restore the purity of Islam, grew up in Algeria under another prestigious personality, Sheikh Ben Badis, who in 1935 formed the Association of Algerian Ulamas.

This demonstration of a renewed Algerian sense of religious and political identity coincided with a transitory revival of French concern with conditions in Algeria, a result of the installation of the Popular Front government in Paris under Léon Blum and a liberal and far-sighted governor-general in Algeria, Maurice Viollette. In 1936 the Blum-Viollette bill introduced into the National Assembly proposed that certain categories of Muslims be allowed to become French citizens without exceptional encumbrances. This would have been a step toward genuine assimilation, but the opposition of the colons, represented by their mayors, the traditional leaders of European protest, was vehement enough to cause the abandonment of any idea of reform.

This failure created disillusionment, frustration, and bitterness among the moderate liberal Algerians who had successfully attained political positions under French rule and who aspired to equality as French citizens. The undermining of Algerian faith in the government strengthened the radical nationalist groups, the PPA and the Ulamas, whose first reaction was to call a Muslim congress, bringing together all groups, including the Parti Communiste Algérien (PCA), which had been established as a separate entity in 1935. However, the unity achieved thereby was brief and superficial.

World War II stimulated the development of Algerian nationalism, especially through the participation of many Algerians in the war, the spectacle of French division and defeat, and the anticipations inspired by General de Gaulle's apparent liberality. During and after the war, Ferhat Abbas, a moderate and respectable politician of bourgeois origins, attained prominence. He was the originator in 1943 of an appeal by Algerian politicians for a constitution guaranteeing basic political rights and freedoms. The "manifesto," which rejected the policy of assimilation that had for so long been supported by moderate Algerians, was "an instrument of propaganda the efficaciousness of which far exceeded the hopes of its authors. It took up the *idée-force* of nation, already launched by the Ulamas and the PPA, and introduced it to a larger public."[4]

The Free French government in Algeria refused the demands made in the manifesto, but in 1944 it promulgated reforms that enlarged the Algerian Muslim electoral college, provided for a two-fifths representation of the Muslims in all elected assemblies, annulled all exceptional laws, and accorded citizenship to certain categories of the Muslim population (estimated to total fifty thousand to sixty thousand people). The opposition parties, which were now united as the "Amis du Manifeste et de la Liberté," in turn rejected these reforms as assimilationist; they vowed instead to work toward an autonomous Algerian republic, although they disagreed over whether it should be federated with France. In sum, the government was offering what the Algerians had wanted ten years earlier, but in the meantime Algerian expectations had escalated. This lag both in the perception of the need to change and in the willingness to do so was a constant factor in French colonial policy.

At the end of the war an event occurred that had profound repercussions for Algeria's political future. On May 8, 1945, in the town of Sétif in the Constantinois district, a parade celebrating V-E day turned into a *bagarre* between Algerian proindependence demonstrators and French police. The riots then expanded into mass Algerian violence against Europeans, resulting in almost a hundred deaths. Of the total Algerian population of the region, less than fifty thousand (5 percent) were thought to have participated in the uprising. Although it was never proved, Messali's PPA was suspected to have been the instigator of the events. The Sétif jacquerie seemed to fulfill the colons' direst predictions of the consequences of liberalization. It was answered by a severe and hysterical repression, which included aerial and offshore bombing of Algerian villages. The official count was fifteen hundred Algerian dead, but a more accurate figure is at least six to eight thousand. Instead of producing abject submission, this excessive force contributed to the growth of nationalism and of hostility against the French.[5]

The shock of Sétif put an end to reform attempts, limited as they had been. The "Amis du Manifeste" was dissolved, and its leaders arrested. A year later, when a general amnesty was proclaimed, Ferhat Abbas founded the Union Démocratique du Manifeste Algérien (UDMA); at the same time Messali returned from exile to establish the Mouvement pour le Triomphe des Libertés Démocratiques (MTLD). The MTLD and the Ulamas refused to cooperate with the UDMA, but it was the strongest and the most popular of the three groups.

Algerian opinion apparently was not consulted about the new statute for Algeria that was adopted under the tripartite government of the Fourth Republic. In 1947, Algeria was divided into departments similar to those of metropolitan France, but with financial autonomy. Executive power was placed in the hands of a governor-general under the direction of the minister of the interior in Paris. He was assisted by an elected Algerian Assembly. Voters were divided into two electoral colleges, the first consisting of the European population and certain categories of Muslims, and the second including almost a million and a half Algerians. The new law also provided for the progressive abolition of the *communes-mixtes*, townships with Algerian majorities in which government was in the hands of French civilian administrators rather than elected officials.

The colons reacted to the 1947 law with hostility. Their alarm increased when the radical MTLD won most of the second-college votes in the first elections under the new system. They blamed the governor-general, Yves Chataigneau, and pressured Paris until he was replaced with the more acceptable Marcel-Edmond Naegelen. The absolute opposition of the Europeans to all liberalization and to any diminution of their superiority meant that any reforms voted in Paris were futile, since their implementation depended on the European-dominated Algerian Assembly. In addition to a voting system that was officially discriminatory, elections were systematically and blatantly rigged under Naegelen's direction to prevent the victory of the nationalist political parties. "In Algeria, electoral fraud is a state institution considered legitimate in the defense of French sovereignty," wrote an observer.[6] Although Naegelen was recalled in 1951, his successor, Roger Léonard, a former police official, was equally firm toward political opposition. No attempt was ever made to abolish the communes-mixtes.

In 1951, the nationalists made another try at achieving unity. The UDMA, the MTLD, the PCA, and the Ulamas joined in an "Algerian Front for the Defense and Respect of Liberty," but their call for free elections had no effect. More significant in the long run was the government's discovery in 1950 of the existence since 1946 of an underground arm of the MTLD, the Organisation Spéciale (OS). It was subsequently destroyed, and in 1952 Messali was confined to the metropole because of his agitation in Algeria. This did not prevent further splintering of the already divided nationalist forces; a split occurred within the MTLD between the loyal followers of Messali and the Central Committee, which resented Messali's personalization of authority and dictatorial methods.

Such, then, was the background against which the Algerian revolution began in 1954. The Algerian masses, now numbering about nine million, had no hope of attaining equality or freedom within the French political system as long as the European population maintained its dominant position. No political reforms were in sight, nor were there plans to develop Algeria, to relieve the poverty and ignorance of its peasants, or to promote social, cultural, economic, or educational advancement. The Algerian population was doomed to permanent inferiority. Although they were discontented and frustrated, the existing Algerian political parties dissipated their energies in internal quarrels that prevented the emergence of a unified opposition. The creation of a new nationalist organization determined to use violence was opportune.

THE FRONT DE LIBÉRATION NATIONALE (FLN): LEADERSHIP, ORGANIZATION, AND IDEOLOGY

Leadership

In William B. Quandt's decisive study of the leadership of the Algerian revolution, the leaders of the 1954 insurrection are typed as revolutionaries, in contrast to the politicians who preceded them.[7] The liberals of the 1930s had been discredited by the futility of their support for the policy of assimilation, and the radicals, centered around Messali Hadj and the MTLD, feared violence because of the repercussions from the Sétif riots. The impotence of the existing parties was exacerbated by internal rivalries and quarrels.

Most of the revolutionaries were men who had been involved in politics before 1954, and had observed at firsthand the failure of normal methods of influencing the system. They had also been members of the OS of the MTLD, and had gained some experience there in the techniques of clandestine organization. According to Quandt, their political socialization, in contrast to that of the politicians, "did not produce a strong desire for modernization and respect for legality. Rather, they seemed much more sensitive to colonialism as an attack upon their own self-esteem, and in reaction they developed intense feelings of their own right to lead the struggle against France."[8]

The origins of the revolutionaries were relatively modest; most came from small towns or villages. Their educations were equally modest, although most (not all) of them had attended secondary school. The politicians (or moderate nationalists) were better educated and had come from more privileged backgrounds. The occupations of the revolutionaries were generally lower in status or nonprofessional. Many had served in the French army (since they were in the age group that had been drafted in World War II); several had even been officers. The French army was a useful source of military expertise for many FLN leaders, including Ahmed Ben Bella, Amar Ouamrane, and Belkacem Krim. The most important aspect of the wartime experience, however, had been its contribution "to a sense of self-respect arising from having successfully competed with Frenchmen and having been fairly treated in the process" and to the stark contrast between the egalitarianism of the French army and the discrimination of the colons, which had been dramatically underscored by the events of Sétif in 1945.[9] At the same time that the Algerian's sense of his own worth and abilities had been raised, his opinion of French power had been lowered because of the French defeat and humiliation both in World War II and in Indochina—that is, the Algerian recognized French vulnerability. The repression at Sétif added further frustration.

Thus, the overall political experience of the revolutionaries had been one of personal failure. Many had sought political office at the local or

Algerian level and were thus victims of the post-1948 electoral fraud that was so commonly practiced in Algeria. Although the efforts of the OS failed under the leadership of Hocine Ait Ahmed and Ahmed Ben Bella, as did another rebellion in Kabylia under Krim, participation in violent opposition gave the revolutionaries a feeling of exclusiveness and an intense commitment to independence through violence. Although most were arrested or exiled in 1950, they remained in contact with each other, and in 1954 they formed the nucleus of the future FLN.

After opening the war for independence, the revolutionaries found that their lack of relevant political experience (particularly in organization and propaganda), as well as their internal disagreements, made it essential to co-opt liberals and radicals into the leadership of the FLN. According to Quandt, the post-1956 alliance of factions produced "leaders with a greater concern for organization and political questions such as authority, representativeness, and public opinion."[10] The political sophistication of the insurrection increased.

As the war continued, the rate of attrition of leaders increased, and new groups were recruited to positions of authority. The most significant new leadership group was the military, whose members rose through the FLN's army. In addition, intellectuals with professional or technical skills rose to prominence through the FLN bureaucracy, which expanded as a result of the expatriation of FLN leaders to Tunis, as well as the later establishment of a provisional government. The political background of both of these younger groups was the war, rather than the colonial period that had influenced both the politicians and the revolutionaries. The military, which gained power as the insurrection progressed, was no more united than the other leadership groups, since it was divided between the guerrilla units of the interior zones and the conventional army, which became a significant force on Algeria's frontiers after 1959 and eventually became dominated by Boumedienne.

Thus the leaders of the Algerian revolution were not a cohesive or homogeneous elite; they belonged to different groups with different interests and outlooks and competed for power in shifting coalitions. Relationships among the leaders were marked by a series of quarrels and crises. The conduct of the revolution was in itself a source of disunity. During the war, these divisions had been rather precariously subordinated to the overriding shared interest in attaining independence. After 1962, however, the rivalries broke into the open until Boumedienne consolidated his power in 1965.

Organization

The direction of the Algerian revolution was originally in the hands of the loosely organized Comité Révolutionnaire d'Unité et d'Action (CRUA), which had been created in the spring of 1954 by the revolutionaries. The president of the CRUA was Mohammed Boudiaf, who relied primarily on five other leaders: Mourad Didouche, Larbi Ben M'Hidi, Mustapha Ben Boulaid, Rabah Bitat, and Belkacem Krim. (By the end of 1957, only Krim and Bitat, of the original six, were still alive, and the latter was in prison.) Ahmed Ben Bella, Hocine Ait Ahmed, and Mohammed Khider composed an "exterior delegation" in Cairo that was charged with soliciting support for the revolutionary forces.

Apparently copying the MTLD's organizational schema, the CRUA divided Algeria into five zones or *wilayas*, plus the Sahara, which was organized later in the war. Ben Boulaid headed the Aurès, Didouche the North Constantine, Krim the Kabylia, Bitat the Algérois, and Ben M'Hidi the Oranie.

For various reasons—including a lack of advance planning and the strength of the French response—the initial FLN leaders paid little attention to the practical problems of coordinating the revolution. In August 1956, a congress was held in the Soummam Valley to reorganize the insurrection. Since the exterior delegation was absent, the interior wilayas (excluding the Aurès, which lapsed into chaos after the death of Ben Boulaid) dominated the conference. The platform of the Soummam Congress established a Comité de Coordination et d'Exécution (CCE) composed of Ben M'Hidi, Krim, Ramdane Abane, Saad Dahlab, and Benyoussef Benkhedda (the latter two radicals). It also established a Conseil National de la Révolution Algérienne (CNRA) with thirty-four members. The platform explicitly stated that the interior was to take precedence over the exterior, and that political interests were to supersede military ones in the conduct of the revolution.

In September 1958, after the establishment of the Fifth French Republic, and the removal of the leadership of the revolution from Algeria to Tunis, the CCE was replaced by the Gouvernement Provisoire de la République Algérienne (GPRA), whose first president was Ferhat Abbas, succeeded by Benkhedda. However, the real power lay with shifting factions of the CNRA, particularly the military.

In the interior, the leader of each wilaya was a colonel in the Armée de Libération Nationale (ALN), the military counterpart to the FLN.[11]

Beneath his considerable authority were three assistants, one for political affairs, one for military affairs, and one for liaison and intelligence. This tripartite division of responsibility was repeated in the subordinate echelons of the wilaya organization. The structure of the ALN's
guerrilla bands (*moudjahidin*) was modeled on that of the French army,
with companies, battalions, and so forth.

The assistant for political affairs of the wilaya was in charge of
financial matters, propaganda, and, most important, the Organisation
Politico-Administrative (OPA). The OPA was the clandestine FLN
structure at the local or village level that served as a parallel administration to the French one. Under the authority of the wilaya's political
assistant, the local OPA or countergovernment was directed by a committee of three, consisting of a president, a political assistant, and an
administrative assistant.

In the Algerian cities, the OPA was adapted to urban life. Authority
was more decentralized, and ALN commandos were attached to the
organization at fairly low levels. The military chiefs were the equivalents
of the political assistants in the committees of three in the village OPAs.
In 1956, the city of Algiers was set up as the Zone Autonome d'Alger
(ZAA), under the direct control of the CCE. The ZAA was divided into
three regions, and into smaller sectors, subsectors, quarters, groups, and
cells. The structure was a typical triangular cellular arrangement,
designed to preserve anonymity and security. In January 1957, the
French estimated that between 750 and 1000 militants were organized in
the ZAA.[12]

The "military" activities of the ZAA—that is, those involving violence—were under the control of the ALN, which was headed by Saadi
Yacef during the period of the Battle of Algiers (1956–1957; see
table 1). The central direction of the ALN administered separate sections for bombings, attacks on police, and logistics, as well as a "shock
group" under Ali la Pointe. The "réseau spéciale bombes," which was
personally directed by Yacef, was carefully isolated from other ALN
activities. The stages of the process of exploding bombs were strictly
compartmentalized: laboratory work, transportation, storage, distri-
bution, and finally the placing of the bombs in the chosen spots by
"auteurs des attentats."[13] Yacef had no difficulty finding students and
technicians who were capable of making bombs, although their first
products, called "Bettys," were clumsy and heavy. By November 1956,
Yacef had received shipments of plastic from Morocco, and the bomb

TABLE 1

ORGANIZATION OF THE ZONE AUTONOME D'ALGER

CCE

FLN
(Benkhedda)

ALN
(Saadi Yacef)

Bombs

Police

"Shock Group"

Logistics

Region 1

Region 2

Region 3

Sector

Sector

network had begun to develop smaller and more accurate bombs. By January 1957, the ZAA was estimated to possess 150 bombs.

In sum, the FLN/ALN organization was characterized by excessive local autonomy, collegial decision making, elaborate and complex clandestine networks, and an intimate relationship between political and military affairs (the last particularly in urban areas).

Ideology

The FLN did not possess a highly structured or comprehensive ideology; the revolution was simply guided by nationalism. The FLN was willing to accept aid from any source, Communist or otherwise, but it insisted on maintaining its dominance of a flatly non-Marxist movement. Anticolonialism was mixed with an emphasis on revolutionary solidarity among the nations of the Third World, particularly in North Africa, but there was little pan-Arab sentiment. The stated goal of the FLN was the creation of an Islamic state, but the Arabic side of the revolution was played down, probably to avoid offending the Kabyle elements of the leadership (for example, Krim and Abane). Since Algerian unity was both recent and precarious, the FLN emphasized a distinct Algerian identity. The conduct of the revolution was basically pragmatic; little attention was devoted to postindependence problems. Aside from a mention of land reform in the Soummam platform, a natural issue to be raised in a peasant setting, the FLN adopted socialist principles only in 1962. Ideology was not a controversial issue during the struggle; reflection was subordinate to action. In fact, in 1962 the Tripoli Program of the FLN specifically criticized the wartime direction of the FLN for its lack of attention to ideology.[14]

REVOLUTIONARY STRATEGY

The Algerian revolution began on November 1, 1954, with a wave of low-level violence across Algeria. The French reacted vigorously to this show of organized opposition and almost eradicated the fragile FLN organization. From the autumn of 1954 to the summer of 1956, the FLN largely depended on rural guerrilla warfare and attempts to organize local populations in the more mountainous and inaccessible wilayas, Kabylia and the Aurès. The French responded with conventional military operations that steadily increased in amplitude.

From January 1955, to February 1956, the governor-general of Algeria was Jacques Soustelle, an intellectual with a liberal reputation whose views changed drastically as a result of his experiences in Algeria. Recognizing the gravity of the situation in May 1955, the French Assemblée Nationale declared a state of emergency. This enabled the Soustelle administration to implement policies of "integration" (a revised version of assimilation) and "pacification" (which entailed the military pursuit of the FLN). Emphasis was placed on the latter, since security was considered a prerequisite for reform.

It was during this period of the war, as FLN guerrilla activity and violence against Algerians spread at an alarming rate, that more and more liberals and radicals began to opt for the FLN. Messali resisted the attractions of the FLN, however, instead transforming the MTLD into the Mouvement National Algérien (MNA). The rivalry between the MNA and the FLN, sometimes violent, persisted throughout the war, particularly among Algerian workers in France.

In August 1955, the leaders of the Constantinois wilaya led the first mass Algerian uprising of the war, an attack on European civilians that was similar to the Sétif riots of 1945. Again French authorities were provoked to large-scale repression against the local Algerian populations. This combination of bloody and well-publicized events marked a turning point in relations between the European and Algerian communities, resulting in a radical polarization of opinion between the nationalists and the die-hard colons, and a reinforcement of the existing political, social, religious, and ethnic cleavages.

Extremism was further encouraged when European demonstrations in Algiers in February 1956 forced Guy Mollet, the new French prime minister, to rescind his nomination of a resident minister who was reputed to be sympathetic to the nationalist cause. This surrender to ultra European pressure undermined the new Socialist government's promises of reforms leading to peace in Algeria and increased the Algerian nationalists' lack of confidence in anything other than a violent solution.

Soustelle's successor was Robert Lacoste, a man of unquestioned loyalty to his government and his party but of little imagination or dynamism. During his term of slightly more than two years, rural insecurity spread despite increasing French troop commitments (the force numbered four hundred thousand by 1957). The predominantly European coastal areas, even Algiers and its suburbs, experienced violence, and the delegation to the government of special powers to act in

Algeria did little to augment the efficiency of the conventional military response.

It was at this point in the insurrection that the FLN held its first conference in the Soummam Valley in August 1956. Any reaction from the absent exterior delegation to the decisions that were made there was forestalled when in October 1956, French military authorities seized the airplane on which its members were passengers, thus removing a source of rivalry to the existing FLN leadership.

In accordance with specific authorization given to it at Soummam and under the direction of the CCE in Algiers, in September 1956, the ZAA opened a campaign of mass-casualty bombings of European civilians, as well as selective assassinations of prominent supporters of the regime, both Algerian and European. The Europeans responded with anti-Algerian violence, and a climate of extreme insecurity and fear prevailed. Under such tense and volatile circumstances and in the face of a threat by the FLN of an eight-day general strike that would paralyze Algiers, Lacoste delegated the responsibility for maintaining order to General Jacques Massu and his 10th Paratroop Division (following a precedent established in other regions of Algeria of the abdication of civilian authority). The Battle of Algiers between the ZAA (particularly Saadi Yacef's ALN) and the French paratroopers began when the army effectively broke the strike. However, Massu found it impossible to halt ALN violence except through the use of extremely brutal measures, including the torture of suspects.

As French pressure mounted, the CCE fled Algiers, although Ben M'Hidi was captured by the French and killed. In September 1957 Yacef was also captured, and the Battle of Algiers was over.

After its arrival in Tunis, the CCE became embroiled in internal quarrels from which the military emerged as the most powerful faction. Dissent was dealt with summarily. In early 1958, Abane was apparently executed, and later in the war a plot by lower-level ALN officers was quashed and its leaders executed.

In 1957, again implementing a decision made at the Soummam Congress, the FLN expanded its operations into metropolitan France primarily in an attempt to win over Algerian workers from the MNA. The number of Algerian deaths in France in 1957 was more than ten times greater than it had been in 1956.[15] The Fédération de France du FLN (FFFLN) became the major source of funds for the revolution.[16]

The frustration of the French army and the Europeans in Algeria over the conduct of the war contributed to the fall of the Fourth Republic in May 1958. These groups blamed the government for its instability and lack of resolution in failing to take advantage of the army's gains, especially after the completion in early 1958 of the "Morice Line" on the Algero-Tunisian frontier cut off the flow of foreign arms to the wilayas of the interior.[17] Since the fall of the Mollet government in May 1957, political crises had produced ever longer stalemates in Paris. On April 15, 1958, the issue of French bombing of FLN sanctuaries in Tunisia at Sakiet Sidi-Youssef finally brought down the next-to-last government of the Fourth Republic. Fearing abandonment if a government favoring direct negotiations with the FLN were approved, Algeria's Europeans formed an uneasy alliance with the army, who had a vested interest in victory and distrusted the politicians, whom they blamed for the French defeats in Indochina and at Suez.

The May 13 revolt in Algiers brought de Gaulle back to power, but the Fifth Republic proved much less susceptible to interest-group pressures than the Fourth Republic had been. Although de Gaulle vigorously supported the military effort in Algeria, he was determined to negotiate a political solution. The implementation of the Challe Plan (named after the new commander-in-chief, Maurice Challe), a successful campaign of broad area sweeps with concentrated forces, was probably intended to strengthen the French bargaining position, not to maintain colonial rule.

The FLN responded to the constitution of the Fifth Republic with the creation of the GPRA. Despite the unfavorable military situation in Algeria, the GPRA consistently refused to compromise its objective of total independence or to permit the inclusion in negotiations of any other Algerian parties. Cease-fire offers and invitations to participate in elections were rejected. The FLN attempted to enforce Algerian noncooperation with the French administration in any form. Although the French had severely restricted the scope of ALN activity, sporadic low-level violence was enough to keep Algeria in a state of insecurity. Meanwhile the nationalist cause steadily gained international support. However, morale was very low among the ALN of the interior, and the military faction affiliated with the army of the exterior was becoming increasingly intransigent.

European hostility and frustration again erupted into open opposition to the central government in January 1960. A European activist demonstration resulted in the erection of barricades and a prolonged siege. Ultimately resolved to the benefit of the de Gaulle government, the

"Barricades Affair" helped de Gaulle to harden his stance against conservative and military pressures to maintain "Algérie française."

The first negotiations between the French and the FLN took place in June 1960 at Melun. De Gaulle's intractability apparently caused their failure, but he later adopted a more conciliatory position and resorted to the characteristic tactic of a referendum on a proposed policy of self-determination for Algeria. The January 1961 referendum vote, which was preceded by violent proindependence demonstrations in Algeria, was favorable, and it seems fair to conclude that from this point on, as far as de Gaulle and the GPRA were concerned, Algerian independence was no longer an issue. Only the conditions governing relations between the future Algerian state and France really remained to be settled.

De Gaulle's intentions were further demonstrated by a unilateral truce that was implemented in Algeria in March. This reprieve permitted the leaders of the interior wilayas, who refused to honor the truce, to regroup their forces. In April de Gaulle proposed the partition of Algeria (probably only as a pressure tactic to force the GPRA to come to terms). Ten days later, military resentment of political policy sparked the third European revolt in Algeria, the "putsch des généraux" involving Generals Challe, Jouhaud, Salan, and Zeller. Although the revolt failed because of lack of support among the lower levels of the French army, an immediate consequence was the surfacing of the OAS, which had been founded to preserve "Algérie française" by any means. It was masterminded by a group of French colonels, although General Salan was its nominal leader.[18]

De Gaulle's victory over the military rebels reinforced the authority of his regime, and negotiations with the GPRA followed at Evian in May and at Lugrin in July. The talks again foundered, however, as the military faction within the FLN rejected concessions on issues such as control over Saharan oil and the status of the future European minority. In August, Benkhedda replaced Abbas as president of the GPRA.

The stalemate in negotiations was accompanied by random and indiscriminate violence by the OAS both in Algeria and in France. The metropolitan population—weary of the war, disturbed by the brutal image of the French army in Algeria, and irritated by OAS *plasticages*— was eager to see an end to the struggle. But in Algeria, where the pro-FLN sentiment of the Algerian masses was unmistakable, the beleaguered and anguished European population, seduced by OAS promises of the maintenance of French domination, blindly followed it to disaster in a "scorched-earth" policy.

Despite the tragedy and horror of the OAS killings, which the French police and military could not or would not prevent, Franco-GPRA talks recommenced at Les Rousses, finally culminating in an agreement that was reached at Evian in March 1962. The Evian Accords granted the FLN the complete independence and sovereignty it had originally demanded in November 1954.

The OAS responded to this announcement with a destructive but vain attempt to provoke a mass Algerian uprising that would force the French army to intervene to save European lives and thereby sabotage de Gaulle's settlement. Instead the OAS attacks provoked a backlash of violence by the army against Europeans. It was this backlash that spelled the end of OAS power, although special metropolitan police (*les barbouzes*) had also been imported as an anti-OAS measure since the local police were considered untrustworthy.

By the time of the July 1 referendum approving independence, most of the Europeans had left Algeria, although the OAS and the FLN had declared a private cease-fire in June.[19] Some violence and extortion were practiced by irregular Algerian groups that were not under the control of the FLN, but internal order was restored fairly rapidly. After a period of internal maneuvering and bargaining, Ben Bella emerged as president of Algeria, although he was destined to be overthrown by Boumedienne in a bloodless coup in 1965. Since that time, the Algerian state has been remarkably stable; few traces of the violent process by which independence was attained are now visible.

The Concept
of Revolutionary Terrorism

II

DEFINING TERRORISM

The concept of terrorism is both historically and theoretically an inexact one. It has been used to refer to events ranging from the Reign of Terror in the French Revolution and the purges and persecutions of totalitarian regimes to the assassinations, bombings, hijackings, and kidnappings of rebels and revolutionaries. Since there is no commonly accepted definition of terrorism, this analysis begins by proposing one that both corresponds to the reality of the Algerian case and potentially applies to other examples of revolutionary terrorism.*

Revolutionary terrorism is part of the strategy of insurgents who are attempting to gain political power through the overthrow of an incumbent government; thus it has to do with fundamental political change. Terrorism used for this purpose is not an isolated event or a string of random deeds, but a series of deliberate, interrelated, premeditated actions. Thus, the concept of terrorism as it is used in this book does not necessarily include the use of violence by governments to maintain control or to implement their policies.[1]

These individual acts in the systematic process of terrorism are violent; they are acts of emotionally or physically "destructive harm."[2]

*An earlier version of this chapter was published previously. Material from "The Concept of Revolutionary Terrorism" by Martha Crenshaw Hutchinson is reprinted from *Journal of Conflict Resolution* 16, no. 3 (September 1972), pp. 282–96, by permission of the publisher, Sage Publications, Inc.

In its most extreme form, terrorism creates "terror," an emotional state of extreme fear and anxiety.[3] It differs from other instruments of violence because it "lies beyond the norms of violent political agitation that are accepted by a given society."[4] While terrorism must overstep the normal bounds of expression of political and social interests, it may do so in different ways. It often involves acts of atrocious or psychologically shocking violence. Its victims are usually civilians, although they may include the military or the police, and the scene is normally a peaceful one—in which such violence is surprising. The timing and nature of a specific act of terrorism are unpredictable,[5] and its perpetrators are most often anonymous. In mass-casualty bombings, for example, the victims do not know who left the bomb. Nor does the individual victim usually have a personal acquaintance with the assassin. There is no way of knowing in advance who, among apparently harmless fellow citizens, is a potential aggressor. The population is unprepared for the time, the place, the victim, and the attacker; the danger is both arbitrary and unanticipated.

It is primarily this extraordinary character of terrorist violence that distinguishes it from other forms of revolutionary activity, such as guerrilla warfare, which is essentially irregular military activity by organized bands in rural areas. In internal wars, the two types of violence are frequently linked, and guerrilla cadres may perform acts of terrorism, but in method and intent they are unalike. Guerrilla warfare is more utilitarian in purpose, and terrorism is more symbolic.

Acts of terrorism combine the present use of violence with the future threat of it. The physical act itself communicates a threat, although it may be preceded or followed by a more explicit warning. This duality is a result of the process by which revolutionary organizations select their victims. Terrorist targets represent specific groups within society rather than obstacles to be eliminated. Their value to the revolution symbolic. It is here that the question of the "innocence" of the victims of terrorism arises. Although it is often cited as a definitional aspect of terrorism, the problem of "innocence" or "guilt" is in reality a matter of moral perspective. "Innocent" victims are best interpreted as people who have no direct influence on the outcome of the revolutionary conflict.

The victims of terrorism represent or "stand for"[6] certain categories of people, so that violence against an individual member of a group is a threat to all other members of the same or a closely related group. This statement holds for nonhuman or material objects of violence as well; as long as an attack is symbolic rather than utilitarian, it may be part of a terrorist strategy, and this symbolic function contributes to the apparent irrationality and the real unpredictability of terrorist acts. The victim is not necessarily offensive or dangerous to the revolution; he is merely a member of a distinctive group. Although its effects are extremely personal, the act of terrorism is thus doubly anonymous and impersonal since the idiosyncracies of both victim and attacker are inconsequential.

The relationship between terrorist and victim distinguishes terrorism from simple sabotage or assassination.[7] Sabotage and assassination are means of terrorism only if they are facets of a broader strategy. When such acts of violence accomplish in themselves the total objective of the assassin or the saboteur, their political significance is limited. They aim at the removal of a specific person or the damaging of material resources; they are not meant to serve as threats of future violence, even if the motives of their perpetrators are political. In cases of assassination, "the victim must be singled out *as an individual,* not merely as a member or representative of some larger group against which general terrorism is being directed."[8] On the other hand, terrorist attacks are meant to influence a broader audience and to have more profound social repercussions. In a strategy of terrorism, a single act is partial and incomplete; it cannot by itself accomplish the terrorists' goals.

Assassination and sabotage thus differ from terrorism in their limited instrumentality; there are no wider implications and no intended psychological effects on other potential victims. The distinction between simple assassination—the elimination of a specific individual—and assassination as part of a terrorist scheme can be illustrated by the following examples. The assassination by the FLN of Amédée Froger, the symbol of the intransigence of the Algerian colons, was an act of terrorism, but the assassination of King Faisal of Saudi Arabia by his nephew in 1975 was not. This distinction between simple assassination and terrorist assassination was raised during the trial of Ben Sadok, the murderer of Ali Chekkal, a prominent Algerian moderate, during the war. Jean-Paul Sartre, arguing in defense of the accused, insisted that political assassination, an individual act with a precise aim, could not be considered an act of terrorism, which is a maneuver of intimidation.[9] Ben Sadok was not acting on the instructions of the FLN, although that organization later praised the act and attempted to claim credit for it. Sartre was therefore correct when he declared that in terms of intent, Ben Sadok had not committed an act of terrorism.

The reason for these distinctive qualities of terrorism—the extraordinary form of violence and the method of selecting victims—is that terrorists deliberately intend to create a psychological effect. This effect may range from terror among those in the direct audience, among whom there are physical victims, to shock, curiosity, sympathy, or even admiration in groups that are not immediately threatened, that only indirectly form an audience.[10] Terrorism is not always or solely intended to produce the emotion of terror, but it is always intended to have psychological implications that influence political behavior and attitudes. The reaction to terrorism is a difficult factor to calculate, but it is logical, as well as empirically demonstrable, that the most important target of terrorism is the mass of the civilian population of the nation or nations involved, whose loyalties and support may determine the outcome of the revolution.

The essential components of a definition of revolutionary terrorism may be summarized as follows:

1. Terrorism is a systematic and purposeful method used by a revolutionary organization to seize political power from the incumbent government of a state.

2. Terrorism is manifested in a series of individual acts of extraordinary and intolerable violence.

3. Terrorism involves a consistent pattern of symbolic or representative selection of its physical victims or objects.

4. Terrorism is deliberately intended to create a psychological effect on specific groups of people (with the nature of the effect varying according to the identity of the group) in order to change political behavior and attitudes in a manner consonant with the achievement of revolutionary objectives.

The FLN used terrorism as a generalized and intentional method of revolutionary combat during its eight years of struggle with the French. Although it is not possible to prove the precise intent of the FLN (or of any revolutionary organization) in each specific instance, it is reasonable to deduce from the general premise that the FLN's use of terrorism was rationally conceived; that, for example, when the FLN chose Algerian municipal officials as victims, the large number of their subsequent resignations was a logical and desired consequence. The bombings of French civilians during the Battle of Algiers, the assassination of farmers in the Algiers region in 1958–1959, and the killings of Algerians who cooperated with the French are all examples of FLN terrorism. Certain cause-and-effect relationships are provable; for example, in late 1955, following an FLN order forbidding Algerians to bring complaints before French courts, there were so few law cases in Algeria that French judges were only "semi-employed."[11] In most cases, the FLN issued written communications or propaganda explaining its revolutionary activity.[12]

The violent acts that constituted the FLN strategy of terrorism were incontestably extraordinary. A review of the history of Algeria reveals that violent resistance to authority was relatively normal. Among the populations of the Aurès region, banditry was considered an honorable profession. In Kabylia, guerrilla activity had been endemic since World War II without unduly alarming the French. Permanent military garrisons were stationed in the territory because native uprisings were expected. Thus a certain level of violence was apparently acceptable to all concerned, but the limits of this tolerance were revealed in the events at Sétif in 1945. Violence directed at French civilians in the urban and coastal regions was not permissible.

Intra-Algerian violence was much less common than acts of rebellion. against the French. Primitive societies customarily experience much cruelty, but Algerian violence was usually limited to tribal conflict that was ritualized, symbolic, and strictly regulated by custom, and produced little bloodshed.[13] An incident that occurred in the 1930s during an Islamic reform movement led by Ben Badis illustrates the standards prevailing at the time. A reformist journal denounced a Muslim cleric as a traitor and declared that no traitor should go unpunished. Shortly thereafter the object of criticism was murdered, and Ben Badis's most influential and inflammatory lieutenant was accused of incitement to murder and arrested. "Though [he was] ultimately released, neither his morale nor his relations with the fellow-reformers ever recovered from this, and he died, an embittered and relatively isolated man, in 1960. . . ."[14]

The contrast between this scrupulousness and the terrorism the FLN introduced into the situation is dramatic. The relatively small numbers of victims of violence rose to thousands of Algerian dead and wounded. The killing of "traitors" to the organization became common. Before the advent of the FLN, throat cutting had been reserved for animal sacrifice. Mutilation of the face, particularly the nose (the FLN's punishment for breaking the rule against smoking), was made even more horrible by the fact that Algerians regard a person's nose as a symbol of his honor and dignity.[15] In urban areas, bombings, grenade throwing, and machine gunning of crowds were unacceptable to both Algerians and Europeans. Mass uprisings, like the one that occurred in August 1955, or one in Algiers in 1960, were equally intolerable to the European community (not all collective violence, however, can be considered a form of terrorism).

A distinct pattern of victim selection was evident in FLN terrorism; although there were sometimes accidental victims, 'most of them could be linked to identifiable audience groups. For instance, during the Battle of Algiers, the terrorist leader Saadi Yacef apparently made consistent efforts to avoid bombing European gathering places that were also frequented by Algerians.[16] The terrorist victims in Algeria can be divided into several categories: Algerian local or tribal authorities, Algerian officials and bureaucrats in the French administration, members of the rival MNA, Algerians who disobeyed FLN regulations or who cooperated with the French, European or Algerian police, European farmers, French political or military administrators, and the urban European population. Sometimes FLN attacks on material objects were also part of the strategy of terrorism because their purpose was not so much the destruction of material useful to the enemy as the creation of a psychological effect. Burning a farmer's crops or a landowner's forests can represent a personal threat and constitute agrarian or economic terrorism. The FFFLN offensive in metropolitan France in the fall of 1958, in which oil refineries were destroyed, is also an example of sabotage in the service of terrorism.

THE STRATEGY OF TERRORISM

One reason for the prevalence of revolutionary terrorism in the modern world is its effectiveness as a strategy in which the benefits often exceed the costs to the insurgent organization. The publicity given to terrorism communicates this fact to potential imitators. A revolutionary movement's decision to resort to terrorism should be considered a choice among violent means, not between violence and nonviolence. In Algeria revolutionary conditions existed because the incumbent regime had denied peaceful means of political protest. An FLN leader explained,

"Urban terrorism, like guerrilla warfare, is the only method of expression of a crushed people."[17] Despite the propaganda content of such justifications, the absence of normal means of access to the political system and a consequent shift to violence are factors contributing to the choice of terrorism.

Compared with other methods of violent resistance, the cost of terrorism is low. The weakness of an insurgent group may thus make terrorism the only viable alternative, and this is why this tactic is so frequently described as "the weapon of the weak." It requires fewer people than does mass action, a factor that is especially important for groups with limited popular support. A terrorist organization, whether urban or rural, requires only a small number of militants who need little training, no uniforms or supplies, no special equipment such as radios, and limited logistical support, and who do not even need to possess individual weapons. The same weapon may be used for many operations, and a knife is often as efficient as a gun. During the Battle of Algiers, FLN terrorists were usually given their weapons by other militants (frequently women) or picked them up at predesigned dropping places minutes before the attack.[18] A chemistry student can manufacture bombs, even without sophisticated materials such as plastic. Terrorists may often maintain their civilian identities without having to go underground. The basic requirements for terrorism are secrecy, discipline, and strict organization, none of which calls for a heavy investment in money or personnel.

The attractiveness of terrorism to insurgents who lack military power is the reason it often constitutes the first phase in strategic models of insurrection,[19] but these models can be unnecessarily rigid in assigning terrorism only to the outbreak of the conflict. Although the FLN did open hostilities with terrorism in the fall of 1954, its later use, especially after 1959, was a sign of military weakness but not of impending political defeat. Physical or material weakness does not always imply political impotence, and a single-cause explanation of terrorism can be seriously misleading.

The value of terrorism to a revolutionary organization is proportional not to the initial expense incurred, but to its psychological effectiveness. The most extreme reaction to terrorism is the emotion of terror, which supplies both its name and its ultimate shock value. Thus although not all victims of terrorism experience terror, the fact that some do is significant for others. Psychologists commonly define the psychological condition of terror as extreme fear or anxiety. Following Freud, they conceive of normal fear as the rational appreciation of a real danger, whereas anxiety is abnormal fear, an irrational response to a vaguely perceived, unfamiliar menace.[20] Though terrorism is a real, not an imaginary danger, it is a vague, incomprehensible, unpredictable, and unexpected menace—thus it can create a classic anxiety-producing situation. Persons who perceive this threat, even indistinctly, may feel helpless and alone, and thus anxious, but this feeling is often based on *actual* rather than imagined impotence. In many such cases it would be very difficult for individuals threatened by terrorism to avoid it except by taking drastic measures, such as moving out of the country. As David Rapoport has noted:

> The terrorist often deliberately assails the innocent, convincing many bystanders that short of joining the terrorist they can do nothing to eliminate the *possibility* of becoming his victim, too. In maximizing uncertainty he excites extraordinary apprehensions; terror springs *less* from dangers which can be anticipated and thus prepared for, and *more* from those which are so uncertain that our imagination makes them far worse than they actually are.[21]

Terrorism may appear irrational to the threatened individual, who consequently cannot respond rationally. The members of direct-audience groups are vulnerable, and investigations of reactions to air raids have shown that one of the most important causes of anxiety is a feeling of extreme helplessness and the consequent breakdown of a feeling of personal invulnerability. When individuals feel that they have barely escaped serious danger, their psychological defenses are shattered, and they are more sensitive to future threats.[22] Anxiety may prompt those exposed to terrorism to exaggerate their own vulnerability. Studies of concentration-camp prisoners also show that the unpredictability of the danger seems to be the most psychologically disturbing feature of the situation.[23]

Terrorism affects the social structure as well as the individual; it may upset the framework of precepts and images that members of society depend on and trust. The result of not knowing what sort of behavior to expect from others is disorientation. A formerly coherent community may as a result dissolve into a mass of anomic individuals, each concerned only with personal survival.

A social psychologist emphasized the consequences for the individual of the disintegration of the social structure:

No individual or group can stand a sudden and radical overturn of the system of permanences which supports the consistency of any meanings, principles of action, norms of behavior, expectations or memories. Such a *bouleversement* spells madness.[24]

In this respect terrorism conforms to what Chalmers Johnson describes as "antisocial" violence, that is "deliberately intended to prevent orientation and the development of stable expectations" with regard to the system of mutual, anticipated behavior and conventions that guide man's communal existence. "The *sine qua non* of a society . . . is the possession of mutual expectations by members of society, allowing them to orient their behavior to each other."[25] Terrorism may destroy the solidarity, cooperation and interdependence on which social functioning is based, and substitute insecurity and distrust.

The following passages from the personal diary of Mouloud Feraoun, a Kabyle schoolteacher and novelist who was assassinated by the OAS in 1962, eloquently express the effects of FLN terrorism on one individual and his world:

Again a market day. . . . Toward noon I made a rapid tour of the town. People seem tense, ready for any madness, any anger, any stupidity. I felt through the crowd an impression of horror, as though I were living in the midst of a nightmare. An undefinable curse reigns over us. I found myself in the center of the hell of the damned, on which the bright Algerian sun shone. I hurried home, shaken. I do not know where this comes from, this is the first time I feel such suffering. Perhaps that's it, fear, the panicky fear without a precise object, without foundation. . . .

My [French] colleagues are truly mad, they are pitiable and I would like to reassure them. But when one believes himself persecuted, he accepts only scenes of carnage, he thinks only of death. . . .

At each execution of a traitor or pretended such [by the FLN], anguish takes over the survivors. Nobody is sure of anything, it is truly terror. Terror of the soldier, terror of the outlaw. Terror which rules mysterious and inexplicable. . . .

Each of us is guilty just because he belongs to such a category, such a race, such a people. You fear that they will make you pay with your life for your place in the world or the color of your skin, you are afraid of being attacked uniquely because nobody has attacked you yet; you wonder why you don't do anything when you are almost sure of not being able to do anything—even sincerely mourn the victims, mourn them totally in the shadow of that secret and inadmissible joy which is that of the escapee.[26]

While Jacques Soustelle was governor-general of Algeria, he described the effects of terrorism after the August 1955 mass killings in the Constantine area. Instead of stimulating cooperation among the threatened, it led to division and strife. In some areas, shops were closed and people were afraid to leave their homes. Soustelle feared a total collapse of economic life and social structure.[27]

The success of terrorism in producing intense fear is not absolute. Even when they are meant to frighten a direct audience, terrorist acts may produce instead a psychological tolerance or numbed passivity that is often a precursor to hostility and anger, and these feelings may eventually be expressed in aggression toward the terrorists. In some cases, people may become accustomed to living in an atmosphere of constant danger, but in others, the anxiety and frustration they experience may lead them to respond to terrorism with counterviolence. Instead of shattering the social structure, terrorism may instill a new solidarity in a targeted group. The problem, from the viewpoint of both the terrorist and the analyst, is to discover when and why terrorism produces different effects.

In some cases, the revolutionaries may be indifferent to, or even intend, the creation of hostility, notably in direct-audience groups that are disliked by the majority of the civilian population. For example, the anger of the European population was ultimately useful to the FLN. However, although passive bewilderment on the part of the mass population might not be a disastrous outcome for the revolutionary organization, an aggressive antiterrorist reaction from the majority would certainly impair the prospects of a successful revolution.

Two factors may influence the popular attitude toward violence. One is the duration and magnitude of the terrorist danger. Sustained, intense, relentless terrorism may be more likely to cause numbness in a direct-audience group than sporadic terrorism. This suggestion is related to the proposition that a requirement for the success of terrorism is its appearance of unpredictability—it must not become so constant that it is regarded as "normal." Psychologists note than an individual cannot endure a psychological state of terror for a protracted period of time; he produces defenses against the "devastating influence" this would have.[28] He adapts to it so that he can endure or tolerate it. For this reason, it has been suggested that a "more scientific strategy" avoids this effect by employing "waves of terror" with "breathing spells" in between, during which the afflicted population anticipates the next spell of terror:

> It is the latent silent panic in people that makes them into more submissive and suggestible beings. On the other hand, overwhelming fear and acute fright may make rebels of them.[29]

An intriguing psychological study of this "scientific strategy" for violence by an invader against a subject population categorizes terrorism first as "general terror" that is directed against the mass of the population and applied in a series of phases.[30] An initial period of terrorism produces "frantic action" and lowered morale in the object, and the second phase induces a "shaky frame of mind" when the object senses that he is in the center of a storm, the extent and violence of which he ignores. A "fear psychosis" climaxes the third phase, and the fourth stage is decisive: by then the object should be totally paralyzed by fear. At this point the terrorist activity should cease, and it should not be repeated while the memory of the population is still fresh.[31] In contrast, "chronic terror" is a process of steady and repetitive violence to which people become accustomed and thus immune. The object's "will to resist" is liberated, and hatred of the "terror subject" replaces the former inertia. The result is "moral isolation" of the "terror subject."[32]

A third and more efficient method is "enlightened terror," which converts the environment, the normally hostile "resonant mass" of the population, into a sympathetic and "spontaneous assistant" and causes it to reject the government.[33] "Enlightened terror" operates on the premise of "original reaction": an individual will react to terrorism in a predictable manner because his actions will be automatic and unreflective.[34] Terrorism must appear unpredictable to its objects, but their reactions are predetermined.

Revolutionary movements usually lack the power to impose a reign of chronic terror over extensive territory, but in limited areas they may risk a backlash. For example, Feraoun commented about the situation in Kabylia in 1956–1957, a period of intense terrorism:

> For many, all these murders finish by losing their former significance. One wonders, in effect, if all those who fall are traitors. Little by little, doubt and lassitude invade consciences; despair gives way to anger. If this continues each one will accuse himself of treason and all the traitors, reunited, will revolt against the killers, who will expire cruelly in their turn.[35]

There are no known cases of popular revolts against the FLN, but resentment of terrorism may have been the motive for support for the rival MNA or for the village self-defense programs sponsored by the French. The extent of such reactions is impossible to determine.

The second factor in the use of terrorism that may affect the popular reaction to it is the way in which the terrorists communicate with their victims. Psychological studies tentatively indicate that if the revolutionary movement provides its targets with positive recommendations about ways to relieve the condition of stress caused by terrorism, there is less likelihood that they will develop an attitude of "lassitude" or indifference.[36] In the case of Kabylia, the FLN did the opposite: following its usual practice, it forbade the Algerian people to consult doctors, midwives, pharmacists, notaries, judges, or lawyers, or to smoke, drink alcohol, or amuse themselves.[37] These severely negative orders undoubtedly caused widespread frustration, since it was almost impossible to carry out the functions of normal daily life without disobeying them. On the other hand, it does not seem likely that clear and positive recommendations for relief could furnish *complete* release from threat and stress. Compliance with terrorist demands cannot be permitted to buy total immunity; otherwise terrorism would lose its essential attribute of unpredictability. In communicating with their audiences, terrorists walk a narrow line between a clarity that removes the uncertainty necessary to inspire fear and an obscurity that hides the meaning of the terrorist act.

Hostility aroused by terrorism may not necessarily lead to overt aggression against the terrorists. Many psychological theories consider hostility and aggression reactions to frustration,[38] but hostility resulting from frustration caused by terrorism may be "displaced": "Frustrated people often aggress against those they blame for their unpleasant experiences, *but they do not always blame those who actually are most contiguous with these events.*"[39] Since frustrated individuals and outside observers do not necessarily perceive the same "frustrating agent," they may place blame irrationally. People often transfer their aggressions to targets that seem more available and acceptable, less likely to punish them in return.[40]

It is logical for prospective or actual victims of terrorist attacks to blame the government for their vulnerability and insecurity rather than, or in addition to, the terrorists themselves, especially if the terrorists use propaganda effectively to increase the regime's attractiveness as a target of popular aggression and to reinforce their own legitimacy. The Algerian mass uprisings of August 1955 and December 1960 may have been partially caused by repressed frustration resulting from terrorism. The FLN found the task of persuading Algerians to reject the French simpler because of the division in Algerian social and political life between the dominant French minority and the estranged masses, and also because of the brutality of French counterinsurgency methods. By bidding for support as the champion of nationalism and independence (highly appealing although diffuse popular goals) and by vilifying the French "enemy," who seemed to make an effort to deserve such notoriety, the FLN increased the likelihood that popular aggression would be displaced onto the French. The Algerian population may ultimately have feared the FLN more than the French, since they were virtually unprotected against FLN terrorism; thus they reacted against the least-liked and least-feared target.

The result of European mistrust and dissatisfaction with the official response to terrorism was the usurpation of authority by civilian extremists. The government allowed Europeans to form legal armed paramilitary units, but it also tolerated illegal spontaneous crowd violence and organized counterterrorism against Muslims.

If terrorists arouse anger in a potential constituency by their actions, they always have the option of denying their responsibility. During unsettled revolutionary conditions, it is difficult to establish responsibility; opinion is usually so polarized—a condition that terrorism helps to create—that most people believe only the arguments of the side with which they sympathize ideologically; when their preconceived loyalties are strong, they may accept vehement denial as a substitute for proof. The FLN used this tactic occasionally, most remarkably after the 1957 killings at Melouza. On that occasion, ALN forces surrounded a village that had apparently cooperated with both the rival MNA and the French and massacred approximately three hundred male inhabitants. Even though the FLN was certainly responsible for this action and was widely condemned, the Algerian population, as well as FLN militants and ALN guerrillas, apparently accepted the FLN version because they did not trust the French.[41] The government's history of a lack of credibility in relations with the Algerian population aided the FLN.

Ted Robert Gurr argues that terrorism directed against a regime is likely to be successful only when the population is already discontented and basically sympathetic to the insurgents. The disorientation and anxiety experienced by the population may make them turn to the government, not the insurgents. Even in cases in which the regime is too weak to provide protection, support coerced by the insurgents "is unlikely to develop into a more enduring allegiance unless it can be systematically maintained over a long period."[42] In insurgent conflicts one cannot assume the existence of a loyal population, and under such conditions successful revolutionary terrorism, indeed successful revolution, is probably rare. In a situation such as the Algerian war, however, the regime already lacks the active support and allegiance of its citizens; in view of the possibility of displacement of aggression, terrorism seems more likely to drive the population away from the regime than toward it.

On the other hand, Leites and Wolf minimize the importance of popular "hearts and minds." "The only 'act' that R [rebellion] needs desperately from a large proportion of the populace is *nondenunciation* (that is, eschewing the act of informing against R) and noncombat against it."[43] The civilian population need not sympathize with the insurgents; fear, lack of enthusiasm for the authorities, or "commercial" motives that calculate the possibility of reward can be as powerful in prompting behavior as conscience and conviction. Furthermore, since the active supporters of the revolution are always a minority, active mass support is not essential. It is the *behavior* of the "resonant mass" of the population rather than their attitudes or preferences that counts. Thus terrorism may be extremely useful to insurgents even if it only causes the population to deny aid to the regime.

The Algerian case supports the proposition that populations do not act solely from ideological preference. Terrorism can influence attitudes as well as behavior, however. It can polarize opinion: confronted with terrorism, a threatened person can no longer remain neutral or uninvolved in a conflict. As Mouloud Feraoun explained the Algerian situation:

> It is fair however to say that the very violence of terrorism has made no small number among us leave our ease and our laziness in order to reflect. Each one has been obliged to consider the problem, to examine his conscience, to tremble for his skin because the skin of the Kabyle is not worth much in the eyes of the terrorist.[44]

Terrorism also affects the attitudes of members of indirect audience groups; when the victims are members of a disliked minority, violence against them may arouse admiration, pride, and respect in the "resonant mass." Many Algerians applauded FLN terrorism when the victims were Europeans, and many admired the terrorists of the Battle of Algiers as heroes of the revolution.[45] The indignation that the French execution of

FLN prisoners caused in the Algerian population forced Yacef to avenge their deaths by bombing Europeans: "the pressure of Muslim opinion on his clandestine cadres is so strong that they are *obliged* (to manifest their presence and their shared sentiment with the mass of the people) to mark their reaction by an act."[46] Terrorism simultaneously excited fear and hatred in one audience group and sympathy in another, and in doing so it reinforced the prejudices and solidarity of each of the two ethnic communities.

Germaine Tillion, a witness to the cycle of violence and counter-violence in Algiers, described the multiple psychological and political reverberations that terrorism set in motion there. Europeans, maddened by FLN terrorism and tense with fear and horror, called for violence against Algerians to halt terrorism. But governmental repression contributed directly to the continuation of terrorism. The Algerian population, who almost unanimously regarded condemned FLN prisoners as national heroes, reached a state of violent aggression and despair at each execution, (these took place at the prison located near the Casbah). They demanded retaliation by the terrorists even though it would certainly result in even more arrests and executions.[47]

The government response can also prevent the success of terrorism. If the revolutionary organization is weak and lacks active support among the population, official repression may destroy it when the terrorists first announce their existence. This is especially true since repression appears to be more severe in response to spectacular terrorism, such as mass-casualty bombings or assassinations of important people, than to other forms of violence, probably because popular tension and pressure on the government to reply with force are greater. In Algeria, the French army destroyed the small FLN urban organizations immediately after the November 1, 1954, outbreak of terrorism, but they were unable to halt guerrilla activity and clandestine terrorism against Algerians in the countryside, especially in the undeveloped mountainous regions of the interior. Moreover, the events in Algeria indicate that if the regime's antiterrorist measures are ineffective, repression may further the revolutionary goals by alienating the civilian population from the government and creating sympathy for the revolutionaries.

A revolutionary organization can to some degree predict a regime's response to terrorism by considering the history of its reactions to crises and its present policy commitments and preoccupations. The French in Algeria had consistently reacted forcefully to Algerian political opposition, whether peaceful or violent. In 1954 the FLN risked provoking another massive repression like the one at Sétif in 1945, but the time seemed ripe for revolt. The unwieldy and *immobilist* Fourth Republic was burdened with the Indochina defeat, the problems of the European Defense Community, and, above all, nationalist agitation in Tunisia and Morocco. Most of the professional army was still in Indochina. It was thus unlikely that the government would have the resources to restore order efficiently or thoroughly.

An analysis of the relative advantages and disadvantages of the use of terrorism must consider the question of its consequences for the insurgents themselves, in personal and in organizational terms, as well as its effects on outside audiences. Frantz Fanon's well-known approach to the subject, which is based on his experience with the FLN during the Algerian revolution, views violence as therapeutic and beneficial, a "cleansing force": "it frees the native from his inferiority complex and from his despair and inaction; it makes him fearless and restores his self-respect."[48] A former FLN leader, Amar Ouzegane, agreed that "terrorism functioned as a safety valve."[49] It served as a means of psychological liberation from French rule, of individual self-control, and of organizational discipline by relieving militant impatience and tension.

According to Fanon, violence also binds the individual to the revolutionary cause; the confidence of the FLN leaders in their subordinates was "proportional to the hopelessness of each case. You could be sure of a new recruit when he could no longer go back into the colonial system."[50] These bonds in turn served the needs of individuals, especially by integrating them into a new community that provided freedom from the colonial system, in which the "native" was always alienated.

Philippe Ivernel, a critic of these theories, noted that Fanon, as a psychologist, listed cases of Algerians who had been traumatized by having suffered French violence and that French physicians could add cases of French who had been traumatized by having killed or tortured. Instead of having a "disalienating effect," violence is a traumatizing factor that results in a fatalistic repetition of violence. Thus the violence the French had suffered at the hands of the Germans was echoed in Indochina and then in Algeria. The first terrorists of 1954 were the sons of those who had been shot in 1945.[51] Violence condemns those who experience it to repeat it forever. Ouzegane, however, might object that "one must differentiate between 'violence which liberates and violence which oppresses.' "[52]

Although it is correct that the events at Sétif greatly influenced the 1954 movement, the theory of traumatization can be challenged. Many French who suffered from the Nazis were sensitized to violence, not numbed to it, by their experience. Several of them, for example, Germaine Tillion and General Jacques Pâris de Bollardière, tried to halt the spiral of violence in Algeria.[53] It is difficult to draw general correlations between the experience of violence and subsequent attitudes toward its use.

Other studies also seem to dispute Fanon's theories. Janis and Katz, for example, described three "corrupting effects" of violence: guilt, the weakening of internal superego controls, and "contagion effects," unrestrained imitation among members of the group. As violence becomes a habit, recourse to it becomes more likely, more extreme, and less controllable.[54] According to Franz Neumann, who corroborates Fanon's conclusions but not his reasoning, violence causes guilt that encourages future violence by reinforcing the solidarity of the members of the revolutionary organization. To bind the terrorists to himself and to the ideals of the revolution, the leader orders the commission of acts that are criminal in terms of the established political and social order, but moral in the eyes of the revolutionary movement. The neurotic anxiety that his followers then experience makes them psychologically dependent on their sense of identification with the revolutionary movement.

The repression of guilt results in near-panic that can only be resolved by complete surrender to the will of the leader.[55] The conflict between deeply instilled normative values and the performance of acts that can be intellectually but not emotionally justified is beneficial to the organization, but not to the individual.

Revolutionary leaders, such as Ouzegane, treat the moral problem of terrorism as one in which the ends justify the means. They consider terrorism a last resort in an attempt to express political opinion and thus a measure of desperation that has been provoked by the regime. "It's our only way of expressing ourselves," explained Yacef.[56] That these justifications do not always exorcise guilt is shown by the fact that FLN members are known to have shown emotion over the deaths for which they were responsible. Yacef, who disguised himself as a woman to inspect the results of a bombing he had ordered, was profoundly upset when he discovered the body of a European friend. He wept when Germaine Tillion reminded him of the deaths he had caused and when she called him an assassin.[57] One member of the Algiers bomb network,

Djamila Bouazza, was mentally unbalanced by having caused the death of someone who resembled her grandmother, although some observers considered her insanity a pretense.[58] A bomb maker, Taleb, also had moral qualms; he left Algiers and joined the maquis when he learned that the FLN leaders had not kept their promise to use his bombs only for material targets.[59] (Colonel Godard disputes the accuracy of this view and insists that Taleb was actually the brains behind the bomb network.) However, another terrorist, Zohra Drif, who was apparently less sensitive, described the role of the terrorist as no different from that of the technician or the soldier.[60]

Whether or not a terrorist experiences guilt is a matter of individual psychology; there is no "terrorist personality." Nor is there evidence that the psychological effects of terrorism have long-term consequences for the terrorists themselves or for the society of which they form a part. The Algerian terrorists have apparently found no difficulty integrating themselves into the postrevolutionary society. Zohra Drif, for example, became an attorney and is the wife of Algeria's minister of transportation, Rabah Bitat. Any discernible results of violence do not seem to be attributable to terrorism per se. For example, the instigators of the sporadic armed opposition to the Ben Bella and Boumedienne regimes in the 1960s were former ALN guerrilla leaders. A general weariness with violence and insecurity led to popular demonstrations against the factional strife of the early period of postwar political consolidation.

To sum up, terrorism's attractiveness and its frequent use by revolutionary organizations are due to a combination of economy and facility of means and high psychological and political effectiveness. From the revolutionary viewpoint, there are certain foreseeable risks in a terrorist strategy: (1) failure to produce psychological fear and instead the creation of hostility in the "resonant mass"; (2) provocation of governmental repression that may destroy the incipient revolutionary movement; and (3) harmful emotional reactions in the members of the revolutionary organization or damage to the future society the revolution is attempting to create. The first of these potential obstacles to effective terrorism may be overcome by skillful use of propaganda and communication. It is difficult to conceive of a situation in which a nongovernmental minority, using terrorism, could impose an unpopular solution on a hostile majority, even if that majority were threatened; in effect, successful terrorism uses unacceptable means to further a policy that is acceptable to the masses. The second hindrance, the regime's reaction, is external to the revolutionary movement, but it can be accounted for in the calculations of the insurgents. If the revolution is seriously bidding for mass support, governmental repression, especially if it is indiscriminate and inefficient, may aid it in the long run. The insurgents can ignore the third problem since it has not been proven that terrorism permanently harms its practitioners. Communications that justify terrorism on moral grounds may also offset any ill effects. Paradoxically, terrorism, which often appears irrational or unpredictable—an image that may contribute to its political effectiveness—is basically a rational revolutionary strategy, in the sense of being a reasonable political choice. Terrorism is a policy that entails foreseeable costs and benefits. The terrorism of the FLN was the result of deliberate decisions by the revolutionary elite, not, in most cases, a pathological or irrational outburst.

THE USES OF TERRORISM IN REVOLUTION

To a revolutionary organization, the benefits of a strategy of terrorism are related to the political objectives such an action can achieve and the likelihood that they will be accomplished. The significance of individual acts of terrorism depends on the function they serve in the revolution. A classification of terrorist acts according to political purpose will help to clarify the concept of terrorism and will provide a method for ordering the data on terrorism.

Thomas P. Thornton has proposed a general typology of acts of terrorism, based on short-run goals or "proximate objectives" of the activity. In his classification model, each act possesses "tactical considerations," which include the target to be affected, the response of the target, and the degree of discrimination in the selection of victims. The target (or audience) may be the victim, his "identification group," the "resonant mass," or the terrorist movement itself. The possible responses are enthusiasm, fright, anxiety, or despair. Thornton considers disorientation, "the destruction of the social framework, so that the individual perceives himself to be alone in his anguish even though he may be physically undisturbed," to be the objective par excellence of terrorism.[61]

A more satisfactory framework of analysis would be broader than Thornton's model, which is limited to the secondary or intermediate objectives of terrorism, while the significance of the strategy lies in its relationship to the general revolutionary goals that these "proximate

TABLE 2
TYPOLOGY OF ACTS OF TERRORISM

Proximate Objectives	Tactical Considerations		
	Target	Response	Discrimination
Morale building	Sympathizers	Enthusiasm	Irrelevant
Advertising	Mass	Curiosity	High
Disorientation	Mass	Anxiety	Low
Elimination	Victim and identification group	Despair and immobility	High
Provocation	Identification group	Fear	High

objectives" serve. Such a framework, based on a set of general categories, should incorporate the complex detail of reality while emphasizing the common factors of each basic function of terrorism. The analyst would thus have the difficult task of combining abstraction and simplification with comprehensiveness and relevance.

The political objectives of the FLN were clearly and directly set out at the 1956 Soummam Congress. The two fundamental aims of the FLN were to obtain the absolute and uncompromised independence of Algeria from France and to establish the FLN's position as the *seul interlocuteur valable,* the unique representative of the nationalist viewpoint and the only agent entitled to negotiate with the French on behalf of the Algerian people. These ends encompassed the following general political goals: (1) gaining the support of the Muslim population; (2) isolating and weakening the French in Algeria; (3) impressing the struggle on the French metropolitan population and obtaining support from its liberal elements; and (4) making the conflict an international issue. In addition, FLN terrorism served internal needs, which remained private: it was used both to maintain the coherence and discipline of the organization itself and to alter the balance of power among rival factions within the FLN leadership.

To develop a comparative study of terrorist activity within the context of the Algerian revolution, it is essential to ask the same questions about each of the types of terrorism, which are distinguished by political purpose. The questions must also be relevant to an explanation of the causes of terrorism and the process of violence, as well as its results. The following set of four basic questions can be applied to each general class of acts of terrorism: (1) What were the FLN's specific objectives in using this form of terrorism? (2) Who were the audiences for terrorism and how did they react? (3) How did the physical process of terrorism work? (4) Did this form of terrorism generally succeed or fail in accomplishing the political goals set by the FLN?

The revolutionary organization's objectives in using terrorism are at the center of the analysis, but definitive information on revolutionary motivations and intentions is hard to come by. Revolutionary organizations operate under conditions of secrecy, haste, and tension. They lack a regularized bureaucratic apparatus, an ordered hierarchy of authority, or clear and efficient channels of communication. The FLN case demonstrates that divided leadership, decentralization, extensive local autonomy, blurred lines of authority and responsibility, and poor, often sporadic, lines of communication are closer to reality. These decision-making conditions make it easier for a faction of the revolutionary organization (such as the military) to gain preponderant power than for a corresponding department in a normal government operating under traditional, formal, and legal restraints to do so. They also facilitate independent and uncoordinated decision making by provincial leaders. Whether it is centrally or locally directed, terrorism may be a destabilizing factor in the revolutionary organization because it is a source of internal controversy.

The presence or absence of communication by the insurgents to the public may help to explain the objectives of terrorism. Communication may link intent and result, especially when it takes the form of a denial of responsibility for a particular action, but the revolutionary organization may also explicitly accept responsibility for acts, either through prior warnings to potential victims or through claims made after the fact. Propaganda statements frequently relate terrorist acts to revolutionary ideology and explain the choice of target or the desired result.

The identification of the group of people a terrorist attack is meant to affect is a crucial factor in explaining the motivation of the terrorists. A direct audience is the victim's "identification group"; its members are directly affected by the act of terrorism because they, as potential victims, are personally threatened. An indirect audience is not intimately affiliated with the victim; its members are one step removed from the threat.

The response of the selected audience is equally important. It can be described in terms of the emotions evoked by the act—terror, fear, shock, alarm, curiosity, respect, admiration—and the political reaction. The political response may be the performance of a particular action demanded by the terrorists (material assistance or a resignation from office, for example) or a genuine shift in political attitudes (for instance, from unconcern or neutrality to sympathy). Questions about audience and response are also important in evaluating the effectiveness of terrorism since there may be discrepancies between the groups the terrorists meant to affect and those who were actually influenced.

The means of terrorism, which may be termed the instrumental considerations of the action, include, first, the identities of the victims of the terrorist act. The number of victims affected by a single act of terrorism is also significant; the casualties of such an act usually form the basis for the misleading distinction between "indiscriminate" and "discriminate" types of terrorism. Does the fact that an act of terrorism involved many victims necessarily imply that it was random and unselective? Second, the most obvious aspect of any form of terrorist activity is the tangible, physical form of violence employed, which may be the decisive factor in producing an emotional effect, especially if the attack is particularly brutal or horrible. Some forms of violence, particularly mutilation, are more spectacular or more fearful than others.

Analysis of the relationship between the use of terrorism and the overall military and political strategy of the revolutionary movement is essential to explaining the utility of terrorism. In this context, the factors to be noted include the point in the insurrection at which terrorism is employed—that is, its strategic timing—the chronological duration of a type of terrorism, its conjunction with other forms of revolutionary activity, and its geographical location.

To evaluate the effectiveness of terrorist activity, the analysts must define the intentions of the terrorists and determine whether terrorism accomplished these goals. After determining which forms of terrorism were most successful, it is then necessary to discover the reasons for both success and failure. Terrorism is a revolutionary policy, and all the problems that beset the formulation and implementation of government policy are compounded in the revolutionary setting.

Finally, the analyst of terrorism must remember that "an economically-minded insurgent group will attempt to make each act effect as many objectives as possible, and, conversely, the analyst of an act of terrorism should not be misled into thinking that each act can have only one objective."[62] The same act may fit into several different conceptual categories simultaneously, and may thus take on different meanings according to the perspective from which it is viewed.

Terrorism and Popular Support

III

Control of the populace is a valuable commodity and a logical goal of revolutionary movements, especially if the conflict is seen as a contest between two elites, the government and the insurgents, for the support of the mass. The FLN gained many concrete benefits from its ability to command at least partial obedience from a majority of the Algerian people. The population was prevented from informing on the FLN to the French during the early years when exposure would have meant disaster, and taxing the people, especially the Algerian workers in France, filled revolutionary coffers. Rural guerrilla bands obtained logistical and material support in their areas of operation and enlisted popular aid in destroying French property, thus compromising the people with the French authorities. Popular participation in strikes, boycotts, and demonstrations (and the severity of the French response) impressed public opinion in Algeria, France, and the world.

The "support," or constructive, function of terrorism includes two conceptually and empirically distinct aims: (1) attempting to secure the compliance or obedience of the population and (2) bidding for sympathy and ideological endorsement. That is, terrorism may coerce support, or it may inspire it. The question is why coercion would be used instead of, or as a companion to, persuasion and propaganda. A population that genuinely sympathized with the revolutionary ideology could better fulfill the functions just mentioned. What purposes could coerced compliance serve that sympathetic endorsement could not? The three possible answers to this question are related to the immediate failure of the initial Toussaint uprising in 1954, decision-making changes within the FLN leadership as the revolution progressed, and the French reaction to the conflict. The initial objective of the FLN terrorism of the Toussaint was to arouse popular sympathy; when that rather modest attempt failed, the goal was shifted to compliance, and the effort to win it continued in different forms throughout the war. But in 1956 the FLN returned to spectacular endorsement terrorism, consisting primarily of attacks on European civilians, a move that had been deliberately avoided up until then.

THE TERRORISM OF THE TOUSSAINT

The primary objective of the Toussaint outbreak, on November 1, 1954, was to provoke ideological awareness and sympathy from the Algerian masses—not merely to secure their obedience, but to enlist their active aid in the struggle against the French. The CRUA made this decision unanimously and communicated it throughout the organization, small as it was at that time. A statement drawn up to be released at the same time announced the formation of the FLN to seek national independence in a democratic and Islamic state, with the parallel objectives of purifying the Algerian national movement, liquidating colonialism, internationalizing the Algerian question, emphasizing North African solidarity, and obtaining support from sympathetic nations. The statement also made clear that any means to these ends would be considered acceptable.[1]

Thus during the night of October 31–November 1, 1954, a coordinated wave of more than seventy attacks struck Algeria. These attacks were intended to hit spectacular and symbolic objects such as economic installations and government buildings, police stations and *gendarmeries* (which were both symbols of the government and possible sources of arms), and Algerian notables who had previously been warned to support the FLN and had refused. This was done partially through ambushes of buses and automobiles. It was specifically ordered, however, that under no circumstances were European civilians to be harmed.[2]

It would thus seem that the relevant audience groups, in order of importance, were: (1) the mass population of Algerians; (2) the European population of Algeria and the French government; (3) the metropolitan population; and (4) the Arab states, particularly Egypt, the most likely to furnish some sort of aid. The only direct audiences were the French government and to a lesser extent the Algerian elite, who were supported by the French authority structure. The intended responses of these groups (in the same order) were: (1) enthusiasm and spontaneous adherence to the cause of independence; (2) shock, fear, and realization that the FLN was a force to be reckoned with; (3) a similar response, but perhaps with less fear and more awe; and (4) attention, pride, sympathy, and aid. In all cases the reactions were to be both attitudinal and behavioral—that is, the FLN seemed to expect both a change in viewpoint and some active change in behavior.

There was, however, a serious divergence between the FLN's objectives and the consequences of its terrorism. Many attacks failed to materialize because of lack of arms or of cadres. The FLN initiated its series of attacks with extremely modest means, certainly less than eight hundred men, around four hundred small arms (most of them left over from the days of the OS, and a few homemade bombs.[3] The attacks generally caused very little material damage. For example, a bomb meant for oil tankers in the Algiers harbor failed to explode. Altogether the attacks took seven victims; the most significant results were in the Aurès Mountains, where the FLN isolated an entire town for more than twenty-four hours and a gendarmerie for a period of time.

Moreover, there were two accidental victims (that is, people who were not targeted by the FLN leadership): a French schoolteacher, Guy Monnerot, and his wife, who were involved in the ambush of a bus in the Aurès. Guy Monnerot was killed and Madame Monnerot wounded.

The audience responses did not approach the FLN's expectations. The Algerian population, horrified at Guy Monnerot's death and afraid of French retaliation, retreated into even deeper apathy and passivity than before. Most Algerians reacted with curiosity mixed with incomprehension, although the younger generation was more impressed. An FLN militant later reported that the traditional political cadres of Algeria were more anxious about the French repression they knew would follow than about the cause of independence.[4] In fact, some members of the population subsequently aided the French against the FLN.[5]

Algeria's Europeans were only slightly impressed with the coordination of the attacks over the wide expanse of Algerian territory. This evidence of central planning did not change their general view that the best way to deal with political opposition was to meet force with force. The police and a French military establishment of about fifty-six thousand men responded with efficient repression, soon destroying the urban FLN organizations in Algiers and Oran. The government played into the FLN's hands, however, by banning the rival nationalist MTLD and arresting its members, many of whom went over to the FLN when they were released from prison.

Metropolitan France was scarcely troubled by the news of violence in Algeria and the announced creation of a new nationalist movement. Nor was significant international aid forthcoming because of the events of the Toussaint. Nasser tolerated the FLN mission in Cairo (of which Ben Bella was a member), but that was all.

In the case of the Toussaint attacks, violence was accompanied by two sorts of communication: prior warnings to prospective Algerian victims and a general public statement explaining the organization's aims. The most interesting aspect of these communications was the FLN's failure to disavow responsibility for the killing of Monnerot, even though it had been carried out against orders.[6] Although the absence of an explanation for his death may have been an oversight resulting from the disorganization and confusion brought about by the French response, the acceptance of responsibility for such acts became the FLN's standard practice.

The extreme discrepancy between objective and results, in what was essentially a case of terrorism aimed at acquiring popular endorsement, was one cause of the switch to compliance terrorism against largely rural populations in the following years. This tactic was used especially in 1954–1957, but it continued, along with new forms of endorsement terrorism, throughout the war. The disappointment over the popular response to the Toussaint attacks influenced FLN decision making. Extremely vulnerable because of the force of the French reaction, the revolutionaries urgently needed at least popular neutrality, but their only means of preventing the population from betraying them was clandestine coercion. Spectacular terrorism that is intended to obtain endorsement requires greater organization, planning, and strength than does clandestine compliance terrorism, and the direction of the FLN was no longer centralized; it was fragmented and uncoordinated. Thus the initial turn to compliance terrorism was almost a spontaneous reaction to circumstances rather than a planned policy.

Paradoxically, the nonconciliatory French attitude to the nationalist movement led to the FLN's almost exclusive reliance on compliance instead of endorsement terrorism during the first two years of the war, as well as its later shift to endorsement terrorism after the Soummam conference in the summer of 1956. Repression first forced the FLN to concentrate on the bare requirements of existence, but encouraged it to broaden its base of popular support after many Algerians were alienated from the government by French violence.

COMPLIANCE TERRORISM

In view of the difficulties of the FLN position, the degree of organization its leaders managed to achieve in the period 1954–1956 was surprising. The implantation of the OPA at the local level enabled the FLN to obtain a high degree of compliance from rural populations. One of the OPA's preferred means of enforcing control over a village was to forbid drinking alcohol, smoking, and amusement. These rules reflected a certain Islamic puritanism, a desire to boycott French products, and a means of asserting its authority over the population. Once the OPA had established discipline in a village, uniformed ALN guerrilla bands, who lived apart from the population, would enlist the inhabitants as auxiliaries, or *mousseblin*. Through the spread of such imperceptible networks of influence, the FLN expanded through the Aurès, Kabylia, and the North Constantinois area. By the middle of 1956 there were probably several thousand ALN soldiers.

An excellent illustration of the FLN's rural strategy and the place of terrorism in it is a directive issued by Belkacem Krim, one of the *chefs historiques* and the commander of the Kabylia wilaya (where he had led guerrilla bands since World War II). During the first ten days of July 1955, the ALN soldiers were to enlist the aid of local peasants in destroying roads and bridges, cutting telephone lines, ruining European crops, and liquidating "traitors." During the next ten days, ALN units were to attack towns, villages, or local markets, where they were to "settle accounts" with recalcitrants. Those who had disobeyed orders not to smoke or drink were to be mutilated by having their noses or lips cut off. From the twentieth to the thirtieth of the month, the ALN was to mount ambushes against French troops. It was then to disappear for a week, leaving the population to face certain French retaliation.[7]

Since there was little coordination among the wilayas at this time, the decisions to use terrorism were local, probably made most often at the village level. After 1956, when the unification of the FLN was achieved, these decisions were not usually topics for high-level discussion. They seem to have arisen from a common policy that was controversial only when there were cases of exceptional brutality. For example, the participants in the Soummam conference criticized the Kabyle leader Amirouche for the massacre of all the inhabitants of a village as punishment for supporting the French. The 1955 uprising in the Constantinois was also discussed, and a general warning was included in the summary of the conference.[8]

Compliance terrorism had two basic and direct audience groups within the Algerian population: the existing and potential elites who were rivals for political authority and any "traitors" who disobeyed the FLN and challenged its dominance over the population. Within the category of elites or authorities there were several identifiable targets. First was the Algerian local elite—not an indigenous or natural social and political elite, but one that had been artificially created and imposed by the French colonial administration. In villages, the government rewarded with patronage favors officials such as the *caid,* a local magistrate with police, administrative, and tax-collecting powers, and the *garde-champêtre,* a sort of rural constable, in return for their delivery of votes in a system that was already corrupt and weighted toward the European minority. In towns and cities, municipal councilors, mayors, or other Algerian government officials filled this role. This elite was doubly guilty in FLN eyes since it constituted both a rival Algerian authority structure and a link between the masses and the colonial regime.[9] Also, since local officials were frequently resented by the people, terrorism against them could be a low-risk means of securing popular sympathy as well as compliance.

The FLN wished to acquire the support of the five hundred thousand Algerian workers in France, Germany, and Belgium, in addition to that of the Algerian masses. After the Soummam conference, the CCE decided to bid for the support of these overseas groups, who generally supported the MTLD or its successor, the MNA. One specific group in the category of authorities or potential authorities was the cafe owners in France. The role of the cafe proprietor in the society of emigrant laborers in Europe was a vital one. He acted as banker for the "members" of his cafe, who sent most of their earnings home to Algeria. His influence could be decisive in determining the allegiance of his cafe's members, especially since he deducted from their salaries dues to the FLN or to the MNA. Thus affiliation with an organization was usually by cafe rather than by individual, and cafes were targets of attack.[10]

Another group in this elite category that was a target of FLN terrorism both in Algeria and in Europe was the MNA; it was the FLN's most dangerous rival because of its ideological similarity, its aggressive

opposition to the FLN, and its strength among the population as heir to
the MTLD. The MNA was also the least passive target of FLN violence in
Algeria and in France. Although many of its members went over to the
FLN during the course of the revolution, the MNA remained a constant
threat. At one time de Gaulle offered to negotiate with this organization in addition to, or instead of, the FLN. The MNA even vainly attempted to establish a rural insurgent network in Kabylia in June 1955,
but it had the greatest influence in Algiers and in Europe.[11] Opposition to the MNA or to any other separatist national movement was
essential if the FLN was to achieve its goal of being the unique representative of the Algerian people.

Similar to the MNA but significantly less well organized and with less
active support were those Algerians who were attracted to de Gaulle's
plan for a "third force" with which he could negotiate Algeria's future.
De Gaulle's program of development and political reforms in Algeria
included, for the first time in its history, relatively free elections without
the minority safeguards of previous electoral systems. The FLN reso-
lutely opposed all compromise, and those moderate Algerians who were
hardy enough to become candidates for office or officials in the
reformed system were seen as dangerous indigenous rivals.

In each of these cases, the specific rival authority was a direct
audience, and the entire Algerian population was an indirect audience,
since the purpose of eliminating existing or potential authorities was to
supplant them in their relationship with the people or to prevent their
reaching positions of influence. The FLN hoped that its terrorism would
inspire enough fear in each direct audience to compel its members to
abdicate their roles, abandon their efforts to oppose the FLN, or join the
organization. For example, government employees were expected to
resign. The indirect audience (the "resonant mass"), deprived of leadership, disoriented, insecure, and vulnerable, was then expected to turn to
the FLN for guidance. Perhaps the disorientation created in the indirect
audience was intended as a psychological preparation for subsequent
efforts to gain popular sympathy, but it is doubtful that the FLN's local
leaders consciously thought in these terms. The political responses of the
direct targets were supposed to be primarily behavioral—that is, there
were specific actions that they could either take or refrain from taking—
but only changes in attitude were expected from the indirect audience
(the general population) at the beginning. Other forms of terrorism
were later to influence its behavior.

The victims of FLN violence in this elite category were almost invariably specific individuals—the officials or leaders described above. This concentration of effort was possible because the audience group in each case was relatively small. The form of violence varied: throat cutting, shooting, or hanging. Attacks or assassinations of this nature occurred constantly during the revolution, since the FLN was very sensitive to challenges, and these acts seem to have had little strategic significance; they accompanied any FLN policy. The attacks were isolated in that they occurred singly rather than in great waves that would receive a great deal of attention or publicity, but the consistency of this type of violence in time and over geographical regions meant that it became a permanent and almost commonplace feature of the revolution. Almost any random account of FLN violence in Algeria listed among the victims a caid, a garde-champêtre, a mayor, or a municipal councilor. This systematic terrorism probably reached peaks of frequency when the FLN first began organizing an area or when there was a possibility of some political change that might increase the influence of rival groups, such as elections in which Algerians could participate as candidates.

The FLN also enforced obedience with direct attacks on the "resonant mass" of the Algerian population. The desired psychological response was apparently classic insecurity and fear, leading to amenability to FLN direction. The FLN wanted the population to be impressed with its strength, determination, and omnipresence. Specifically, it attempted to prevent the population from betraying its members to the French and to force them to aid the organization in acts of sabotage. Victims were usually people who had disobeyed FLN orders, such as the no-smoking rule or other interdictions, but there were so many rules that every Algerian must have felt vulnerable. (Mouloud Feraoun's experiences, which were quoted in the previous chapter, are a vivid example.) The threat of violence was thus both pervasive and continuous throughout the war, and the attacks were often atrocious (throat cuttings or mutilations) and not always individual. There were also bombings and shootings in public places frequented by Algerians, such as markets, cafes, and in Algiers, cinemas. Moreover, there were the cases, although these were very rare and not usually approved by FLN leaders, of mass reprisals against disobedient villages.

The discrepancy between aims and results in compliance terrorism was generally small. The FLN invariably insisted that the victims of compliance terrorism, whether elite or mass, were "traitors." There were frequent warnings of the fate reserved for traitors, and the killers often pinned notes explaining this motivation to the bodies of the victims. Anyone who was not actively pro-FLN risked being labeled a traitor since the FLN did not feel that mere neutrality was sufficient after a certain point. This policy of polarizing loyalties was also a means of legitimizing both the revolution and FLN violence by equating terrorism with governmental punishment of traitors. The FLN thus encouraged acceptance of its authority while it was simultaneously enforcing compliance with its demands through coercion. The habit of obedience that was acquired through compulsion might also have served as a basis for accepting the commands of the FLN as normal and right, particularly since French authority, which was weak among Algerians if not nonexistent, had long ago lost legitimacy.

This meant that FLN terrorism had an ambiguous connotation to Algerians. It was both acceptable and unacceptable. Both the ordinary Algerian and the leader were afraid of FLN violence, for which the surest remedy was to join their threateners. At the same time, the resentment and fear of these potential victims were tempered with the realization that violence against them would be justified to their fellow Algerians. Thus to fear were added feelings of shame and dishonor.[12] Considering the pride and status that could be gained by joining the FLN, it is not surprising that many opted for this solution, and it is difficult to separate actions motivated by fear from those motivated by genuine choice. Although the FLN almost always accepted responsibility for its acts of compliance terrorism, there were exceptions. Acts of particular brutality involving mass victims were repudiated. Responsibility for the massacre at Melouza in 1957, which has already been mentioned, was denied by the FLN, but it seems likely that it was the reaction of an accidental audience group (metropolitan and international opinion) that caused the FLN to deny this action rather than to claim that the treacherous inhabitants of Melouza deserved their fate. There were other cases in which FLN violence was equally reprehensible from a moral viewpoint, but since these incidents received less publicity, the FLN did not comment on them publicly. It was only by chance that Melouza happened to be located in an area that was easily accessible to the press. FLN leaders also refused to admit responsibility for the extortion of funds, although it was undoubtedly practiced.[13]

On the other hand, to publicize the FLN's attitude toward traitors, the organization was not above taking credit for acts that were committed without FLN direction. Ben Sadok assassinated the moderate politician Ali Chekkal in Paris on his own initiative (although he privately sympathized with the FLN), but the FLN immediately claimed responsibility for the act.

ENDORSEMENT TERRORISM

Chronologically, the FLN's use of terrorism, aimed at obtaining popular endorsement—not mere acceptance but allegiance—first followed and then paralleled its use of compliance terrorism. The most significant difference between the two was that in endorsement terrorism, Algerians became an indirect rather than a direct audience; European civilians became the primary victims. The reasons for this policy change within the FLN included the advent of Ramdane Abane as an influential leader in decisions concerning revolutionary strategy, the unification of the organization in the Kabylia and Algérois regions after the August 1956 Soummam conference, and the stalemate produced on the rural front because of the massive involvement of the French army (220,000 troops were committed to these regions by March 1956). French repression also aided the FLN by arousing popular resentment, thereby simplifying the FLN's bid for popular sympathy; the experience of French violence made Algerians increasingly receptive to the nationalist ideology.

In general, endorsement terrorism is more spectacular and more shocking than compliance terrorism. The FLN's version of it encompassed three basic types. The first type, and the one most similar to compliance terrorism, was aimed at inspiring admiration and respect in the "resonant mass." It may also have been meant to prompt the population to action on behalf of the revolutionary movement, as were the events of November 1, 1954, and of August 1955, in the Constantinois. The second type was designed to provoke repression from the government. Spontaneous and indiscriminate violence by French civilians and military against Algerians alienated the masses from the regime, enhanced Algerian solidarity, and increased support for the FLN. It thus served the goals of isolating the French and of gaining popular support. The third kind of endorsement terrorism was a method of satisfying Algerian demands for vengeance against those whom they considered their persecutors. It was closely related to provocation terrorism since

· the violence it elicited from the regime may have caused the population to demand revenge from the revolutionaries.

Undoubtedly because the physical victims in endorsement terrorism were European civilians, the decision to use this tactic deliberately and systematically was the subject of discussion and disagreement within the organization. The August 1955 attacks were an exception, since that decision was made outside the central FLN leadership, but when the leaders accepted the responsibility for that dramatic move, pressure to imitate it mounted. As in the case of the failure of the Toussaint uprising, the FLN was able to learn from past experience, whether or not it was productive in terms of its initial goals.

The events of August 1955 marked a turning point in relations between the Algerian and European communities. In the spring of 1955, the situation for the FLN organization was less favorable in the North Constantinois, near the coast, than in Kabylia and the more mountainous and inaccessible regions. Mourad Didouche, the original leader of the Constantinois wilaya, had been killed in early 1955, and his successor, Zighout Youssef, was apparently isolated from the other FLN leaders. Communications among the scattered FLN organizations were poor. The Constantinois area had been relatively calm compared to Kabylia and the Aurès until May 8, 1955, when a bomb exploded in Constantine, the capital of East Algeria, and Youssef's armed bands attacked gendarmes and government officials. On May 10, they isolated a small town for several hours. The French response to this outbreak was predictably severe—mass arrests, searches, and brutality.

Ignorant of developments in the rest of Algeria, the Constantinois leaders decided that it was necessary to undertake some large-scale action that would improve morale and give the revolution a new impetus. They decided that "collective reprisals against Europeans, military or civilian, all responsible for the crimes committed against our people, should reply to the colonial policy of collective repression."[14] A general offensive was ordered for August 20, the anniversary of the French deposition of the nationalist sultan of Morocco, when the Moroccan nationalists could be expected to demonstrate in some fashion. This attack was to occur in daylight to create the maximum effect, and the FLN assigned specific objectives, such as police stations and government buildings, to ALN bands that were to lead civilians in the attack.

Consequently, on August 20, 1955, tens of thousands of Algerians joined in a frenzied and savage assault with knives, sticks, pitchforks, sickles, and hatchets on unsuspecting Europeans and Algerian "traitors," notably in Philippeville, Constantine, Ain Abid, and El Halia. There were 123 deaths: 71 European civilians, 31 French soldiers, and 21 Algerians, including the nephew of the prominent politician Ferhat Abbas who had recently gone over to the FLN. Forty-seven Algerians, 51 Europeans, and 125 military personnel were wounded.[15] The French response was swift: 12,000 Algerians were estimated dead or missing in the following weeks.[16]

Youssef's principal objective in initiating the August attacks was similar to that of the CRUA in directing the events of the Toussaint less than a year before: to *act* to stimulate the participation of the Algerian population in a mass revolution. According to William Quandt's analysis, the generation of revolutionaries to which the CRUA and Youssef belonged possessed little skill or interest in organization or ideology.[17] Skilled as agitators, they tended to resort to the most direct action possible—violence—when the situation seemed desperate. It was this almost instinctive, politically unsophisticated lashing out in an act of collective peasant aggression that laid the groundwork for a deliberate policy of spectacular, urban, anti-European terrorism. In a sense, Youssef broke a taboo forbidding violence against the dominant colonial class.

Although Europeans were the direct audience of this terrorism, Youssef seemed to be more concerned with the response of the indirect audience—the Algerian population—whose participation, whether willing or coerced, committed it to the FLN, at least in the eyes of the French. Terrorizing Europeans impressed the Algerians. Youssef was also concerned with two other indirect audience groups: an internal one, the revolutionary organization itself, and an external one, the entire North African population, which he hoped to goad into a demonstration of solidarity.

The important question is whether the FLN achieved its aim of obtaining popular endorsement. Although no mass Algerian uprising followed, still August 1955 was "a major event which led many hesitant Muslims to opt for the FLN" and caused the "moderate nationalists" to conclude that "henceforth the FLN must be taken seriously as representative of the Muslim population, which now aspired to independence rather than assimilation or integration."[18] It is interesting that the use of terrorism brought the FLN a representative status that then produced popular endorsement (or at least the two processes were concomitant); endorsement did not confer representative status. By standing out as a prominent symbol, the FLN became representative and gained support. Thus in this case, the discrepancy between intent and result was not detrimental.

The central FLN leadership accepted general responsibility for these events. According to Yves Courrière, Ramdane Abane, who was a major leader at this time, did not approve of Youssef's actions. He considered them harmful to the FLN's long-run interests because they justified French claims that the FLN was composed of fanatical bandits. Abane felt compelled to accept responsibility for local decisions, however, since the FLN had no choice but to allow local autonomy in decisions, and since causing general insecurity was, after all, a major FLN objective.[19]

A significant exception to the FLN's policy of accepting responsibility was the deaths of Alloua Abbas and of Cherif Belhadj Said during the August massacres. Abbas, the nephew of Ferhat Abbas, was a municipal councilor for Constantine; he and Belhadj Said, an attorney, had opened a fund-raising drive for the Association of Ulamas, an action forbidden by the FLN. According to Yves Courrière, Lakhdar Ben Tobbal, Youssef's second-in-command and eventual successor, specifically gave the order to assassinate Abbas. The FLN published a propaganda pamphlet, however, insisting that a serious inquiry had determined that members of the ALN had not killed the two men, who were fellow anticolonialists.[20]

Youssef's deliberate massive attack on European civilians raised the issue of whether the entire FLN organization should use this kind of terrorism; the decision to cover the action, even after the fact, constituted an acceptance of it. This policy was never adopted, however, for metropolitan France, perhaps because the Algerian workers in Europe were more politicized and organized than the Algerian population; they were accustomed to clandestine support of the nationalist cause. Once the FLN had won the battle against the MNA, it almost automatically assumed a position of leadership toward the Algerian constituency in France. The FLN wanted primarily financial support from this group at any rate; a more overt display was not necessary. In addition, since terrorism in Algeria affected the metropolitan workers as well as the domestic population, it really was not essential to risk using endorsement terrorism in France.

To situate this decision to adopt a new form of terrorism in Algeria within the general progress of the revolution, it is important to point out the alternatives that were available to the FLN at that time. It could have either sought the tolerance of at least some part of the European population or treated Europeans as a monolithic enemy and concentrated on gaining Algerian approval. Events, as well as the fact that the nationalist revolution had to confront the colonial system as a whole and could not afford to compromise, drove the FLN to choose the second alternative. After August 1955 and the events of that fall and winter—the French capture of Ben Bella and the FLN's exterior delegation, an increase in extremist European violence against Algerians, Guy Mollet's capitulation to extremist demands in his nomination of a resident minister for Algeria, and continuing military repression—opinion in Algeria was so polarized that the FLN could not have succeeded in winning European neutrality. It is also important to note that the sort of endorsement terrorism the organization now chose was multifunctional in the highest degree. It polarized the conflict, pushing Algerians into the arms of the FLN, relieved the impatience of the militants, created insecurity among Europeans, and weakened the French structure in Algeria.

For present purposes, post-1955 terrorism will be analyzed simply in terms of its function of impressing the Algerian population and acquiring prestige for the FLN. An attack on any European probably sufficed to achieve some response from the indirect audience. Once the revolutionary situation had polarized the European and Algerian communities, neither side made distinctions among individuals. Assassinations of prominent but disliked military and government officials or colons or mass-casualty attacks that received much publicity may have created a sharper response than more anonymous attacks, but there is no proof that this was so.

There is no doubt, however, that the response of the Algerian audience must have included, in addition to respect for the daring of the FLN, an element of fear of French reprisals—a factor that was dominant in the response to ·the terrorism of the Toussaint. Endorsement terrorism had different effects on various subgroups of the Algerian population—tribes from the mountains and deserts of the interior, urban working classes, populations that had been uprooted by the French resettlement policy, young people, women, those who had become politicized, and peasants. Because the population in Algeria was growing rapidly, young people composed a sizable segment of the population; since they were the most likely to be enthusiastic about revolutionary feats, this aided the FLN.[21]

On the other hand, when attacks on Europeans were not specifically motivated by the aims of provocation or vengeance, they probably had as their primary objective the response of the direct audience and of the French authorities, not their effect on the Algerian population. The analysis will now be concentrated specifically on provocation and revenge as objectives of endorsement terrorism, reserving a detailed consideration of general terrorism against Europeans for later.

The provocation of an indiscriminate violent reaction from the regime, from the army, or from European civilians seemed to be a frequent objective of the FLN's terrorism. The polarization resulting from these attacks also isolated the French and increased general insecurity. The value to the FLN of this form of endorsement terrorism was its effect on the indirect audience by means of the response of the direct audience. The fear and anger of the targets of terrorism were expressed in hostility and irrational violence toward Algerians. The French government constituted both a direct and an indirect audience; it was affected by attacks on official victims as well as by violence against European civilians and the army that caused these two powerful interest groups to pressure the government into repression and brutality against the Algerian population. The Europeans in particular, organized and directed by extremist or ultra leaders, possessed exceptional influence over government policy. For example, European pressure on the government to execute condemned FLN prisoners caused the decision to implement capital punishment. The army could also be considered both a direct and an indirect audience, since pressure from European civilians affected it as well as the government. In all three groups the responses were both behavioral and attitudinal: feelings of hostility expressed in aggression.

The instrumental factors vary with each case. For example, there were two types of victims chosen from the European population. First, the FLN targeted prominent leaders of the European community who were symbols of colonialism and of the refusal to relinquish dominant status, such as Amédée Froger, president of the Association of European Mayors, who was assassinated in December 1956. Despite appeals from the resident minister, Robert Lacoste, Froger's funeral occasioned mass European violence against anonymous Algerians in the street.[22] The French police, many of whom were sympathetic to right-wing causes, completely failed to control the rampaging crowds. Second, anonymous European civilians were attacked solely as representatives of that class in what is erroneously called "blind terrorism." This category of victims would include those who were injured or killed in the bombings of European cafes, restaurants, dance-halls, and so on, before and during the Battle of Algiers in 1956 and 1957. For example, after the funeral of the victims of the June 1957 bombing at the Casino de la Corniche, which killed eight and wounded eighty-one, six Algerians were killed and forty-five wounded, twenty cars were burned, and a hundred Algerian stores were pillaged. It could also include the European farmers killed in systematic attacks in the coastal regions, such as the area around Oran; in May 1956, a sudden outbreak of terrorism there left twenty European farmers dead. The problem of protecting agricultural activity, which was constantly menaced by FLN attacks on farms, crops, and rural populations, became a major government preoccupation. In 1955, the Algerian Assembly had voted funds for agricultural "cooperatives," groups of European farmers who had banded together for protection against terrorism, but the Europeans insisted on more protection, and in 1956 departmental prefects were instructed to promote agricultural "syndicates." By thus allowing European civilians to take the responsibility for their own defense, the government encouraged the growth of a powerful and eventually uncontrollable pressure group. In June 1956, Robert Lacoste recognized the problem by blaming the press for exaggerating the numbers of Algerian victims of European violence.[23] Even more serious was the formation of local militia, Unités Territoriales (UTs), which were responsible for much anti-Algerian violence the government was unable to contain. In fact, the FLN terrorism in the Algiers region in December 1959 and January 1960, in which more than twenty Europeans died, was one cause of the "Barricades Affair," which endangered the stability of the de Gaulle regime.

This kind of terrorism seemed particularly useful when the FLN needed relief from French military pressure on its guerrilla troops, but this strategic goal was probably not the FLN's principal objective. These attacks usually occurred in sustained, intense spells that seemed to heighten the effects of fear and anxiety. There were no geographical restrictions except the general immunity of metropolitan France; the geographical pattern was dictated by the presence of concentrations of Europeans in urban and coastal areas.

The most striking evidence of the effects of terrorism on the French government and its administration of Algeria, particularly its attitude and actions toward the Algerian population, is Governor-General

Jacques Soustelle's reaction. Two events apparently caused Soustelle to abandon his belief in the possibility of reforms and a moderate solution to the Algerian problem and to emphasize the military defeat of the revolution rather than "integration." One was the assassination by the FLN of Maurice Dupuy, a personal friend in the French administration of the Aurès region who was well-liked by his Algerian clientele. The second event was the massacre of August 1955, which Soustelle vividly described in his memoirs.[24] The beginning of Soustelle's progression from a liberal faith in reforms to extreme reaction in support of the OAS began in the summer of 1955 when the FLN began the policy of high-casualty terrorism against European civilians.

European bitterness and anger grew when the FLN chose popular civilian or military administrators as targets for assassination.[25] The FLN may have deliberately selected "good officials" in order to provoke the Europeans into violent retaliation and to destroy any basis for compromise between the European and Algerian communities. In addition, Leites and Wolf have pointed out that after insurgents have become relatively strong, assassinating well-liked administrators may increase popular acceptance of the insurgents, who appear powerful and irresistible. These authors have suggested that early in the conflict, while the insurgents are weak, they usually strike at "bad officials"—victims who, in the eyes of the populace, deserve punishment. Such violence is extenuated by the offensiveness of the victim, and it excites popular awe and fear that form the foundation for a later reaction of resignation rather than indignation when the victims are likable or admirable people. Thus FLN attacks on popular French administrators may have been a facet of compliance terrorism as well as provocation terrorism.[26]

FLN terrorism had similar effects on, and met with similar responses from, the French military. Uncontrolled reprisals against the Algerian population were almost as common in the army as they were in the European civilian population. Krim's instructions to his forces in Kabylia—ordering ALN units to disappear after they had performed acts of sabotage and terrorism so that the population would be left to face the French retaliation—are ample evidence that the FLN leaders knew what to expect from the army. In a typical case, in May 1957 in the Le Ruisseau section of Algiers, FLN terrorists killed two paratroopers; in retaliation the comrades of the victims killed or wounded eighty Algerians.

Terrorism to avenge Algerian grievances against the French was closely linked to provocation; the two formed an unending spiral of action and reaction. In this sort of terrorism, the response of the direct audience was not as important as the act itself, because the objective of the revolutionaries was to gain popular support by casting themselves as the agents of vengeance. In a sense, the FLN followed rather than led the Algerian population; it was forced to seek revenge or forfeit respect and honor. Although all FLN terrorism can be interpreted as a means of satisfying unstructured but pervasive Algerian resentment against the colonial power, there are cases in which specific demands were made. It has already been mentioned that during the Battle of Algiers Yacef's terrorist commandos were practically forced to act to satisfy popular calls for vengeance, especially in response to the executions of FLN prisoners that began in June 1956. The FLN may also have sought to avenge European counterterrorist activity. In August 1956, a house was bombed on the rue de Thèbes in the Algiers Casbah, causing at least seventy Algerian casualties. The French insisted that Yacef and the ZAA began planning bomb attacks in the spring of 1956 before the first executions and the explosion on the rue de Thèbes, but the usual FLN explanation is that they were compelled to seek retribution on behalf of these martyrs to the nationalist cause.

On September 30, 1956, Yacef ordered two time bombs to be placed in the European center of Algiers, at the Cafeteria and the Milkbar, which were popular with Europeans. Algerian girls who resembled Europeans closely enough to escape notice left the bombs in a restroom and under a seat. The resulting explosions left two dead and sixty injured. According to both Germaine Tillion and Yves Courrière, Algerians were generally enthusiastic about this action by the FLN. Offended by European indifference to counterterrorism and outraged by the executions of prisoners, they welcomed the FLN retaliation with "exultation" and came to regard the ZAA terrorists as national heroes and protectors.[27]

The FLN always claimed that Europeans were initially responsible for the cycle of violence in Algiers. Mohamed Lebjaoui, for example, insisted that the FLN attacks were only a "tardy reply to European terrorism, legal or illegal."[28] He described the FLN bombings as an "inevitable reply" to the execution of FLN militants and the rue de Thèbes deaths and presented the assassination of Amédée Froger as an act of vengeance for a punitive expedition against Algerians and for the shooting of two Algerian militants in Froger's district.[29]

Vengeance terrorism also seems to have played a role in FLN actions against the OAS in 1961–1962. After the Battle of Algiers, the FLN had abandoned the idea of a ZAA, leaving the Algérois wilaya in charge of activity in Algiers. In the summer of 1960, however, it began reorganizing the zone after the French released some FLN suspects. The new organization was smaller and less rigidly structured than the original ZAA of 1956, but it was also less dependent on the GPRA than the ZAA had been on the CCE. By the spring of 1962, OAS violence had reached an intolerable level of intensity. On May 2, an automobile exploded on the crowded Algiers docks, killing 62 Algerians who had gathered there to look for work. On May 10, the OAS killed 7 cleaning women who worked for European families, and then attempted, but failed, to burn the entire Algiers Casbah. In one week, from May 3 to May 11, the OAS is reported to have killed 230 Algerians.[30] The reaction of the Algerian population to such violence was one reason for the ZAA's transgression of a GPRA order not to respond to OAS violence. According to ZAA Commander Azzedine, if anti-OAS terrorism had not provided a safety valve (despite the fact that it provoked increased anti-Algerian violence from the OAS), the Algerian population would have massacred most of the remaining European inhabitants of Algiers.[31]

It seems that most of the vengeance terrorism took place in Algiers. The population there was more politically sensitive than the peasants of the interior, and it was also subjected to more intense French violence. However, this impression may come from the excessive publicity that was given to terrorism in Algiers, and vengeance terrorism may also have played a role elsewhere. The use of vengeance terrorism by the FLN could almost be called a case of calculated irrationality. The FLN could blame its acts of violence on popular pressure and thus escape disapproval. The victims were members of groups the Algerian population considered responsible for aggression against them. It also seems likely that whereas the most effective victims of provocation terrorism would be popular or sympathetic (in Algerian eyes) members of the direct audience group, the best targets for vengeance terrorism would be the most hated symbols. In terms of timing, vengeance terrorism depended on popular demand, which depended on violence committed by the government, the military, or the European population.

An incident that illustrates the close relationship between provocation terrorism and vengeance terrorism took place near the village of Koléa, near Algiers. The official FLN explanation follows:

> January 22, 1957, the Algiers-Koléa bus was attacked, at 6:30 p.m., by a group of the ALN. The European passengers were executed. After the burial of one of them, a sergeant living at Fouka, the racist militia of that locality kidnapped and killed six Algerians. . . .

Why did the ALN conduct this daring raid and proceed to these executions? The reason is simple. Koléa . . . is the seat of a military school and of a battalion of paratroopers. Before the attack on the bus . . . a grenade was thrown on a paratrooper patrol. During the night they descended to the Arab town "after a loss of control." Led by the territorials, they forced their way into houses that they pillaged before "cleaning them out" with grenades or knives. The number of victims, including several women, is almost sixty. Sixteen girls were raped.[32]

A similar version of the same incident illustrates the general veracity of the FLN's account as well as the variations in detail that plague anyone who tries to establish a definitive record of an event. Abdelkader Rahmani, a lieutenant in the French army who had been imprisoned for protesting French policy in Algeria, remarked that French officials always wanted to talk about FLN "killers" and not about French "killers," but that the killings at Koléa were a reply to a *ratissage* (search) by the forces of "order" several days before in which several hundred Algerians had suffered. Rather than a breach of discipline in response to a grenade attack, the *ratissage* was a deliberate decision motivated solely by the army's desire to "keep their hands in" and to relieve the boredom of inactivity.[33]

All acts in the category of endorsement terrorism, including those aimed at provocation and revenge, appear to have produced little discrepancy between intent and result, with the exceptions of the failures of the Toussaint and the qualified success of August 1955, which taught the FLN some useful lessons. Both provocation and vengeance seem to have been effective uses of terrorism; this is probably why the FLN usually claimed responsibility for these acts, although they never admitted that terrorism might have been deliberately intended to provoke violence. Very general warnings were also occasionally communicated to the direct audience. For example, in May 1958, before the fall of the Fourth Republic, the CCE warned the French that they considered each execution of an ALN soldier, including any terrorists, an "intolerable provocation," and that if the French executed the Algerian students who had been accused of terrorism during the Battle of Algiers, the FLN would be under an "obligation to act."[34] Indeed it was the killing of three French prisoners in Tunis by the FLN in retaliation for the execution of terrorists that led to the demonstration of May 13 that brought de Gaulle to power.

In conclusion, terrorist activity by the FLN to gain Algerian support was generally successful. The consequences of terrorism included both coerced compliance and enthusiastic endorsement from the Algerian people; these two functions of terrorism proved complementary rather than contradictory. A common view of revolutionary conflict assumes that people support a revolutionary movement either because they genuinely sympathize with the ideals of the revolution or because they are intimidated by revolutionary violence. The Algerian case indicates that popular choice results from a mixture of motives, even in a colonial situation where the "resonant mass" is predisposed to welcome a nationalist appeal. It must be remembered that the terrorism of the FLN occurred in the context of a society that was "shaken to its foundation" by the clash between the traditional way of life and colonialism, in a state of disintegration, divided between dominant and dominated classes before the revolution, and suffering during the war under literally catastrophic conditions of displacement, disruption, and deprivation.[35]

It was also significant that despite the apparent inevitability of the revolution, the response of the established government to FLN terrorism was almost completely ineffective in combatting violence against Algerians. That this was the natural response of a colonial regime to violence among the colonized did not lessen Algerian vulnerability and resentment.

Terrorism and the Enemy

IV

FLN terrorism in several forms was directed against all aspects of the French colonial presence in Algeria. The FLN meant to destroy the structure of French domination. The platform of the 1956 Soummam conference described the aims of the revolution as forcing the French, the colonialist enemy, into a cease-fire by weakening the army, causing the deterioration of the colonial economy and the breakdown of French administration, and isolating the French in Algeria. After a cease-fire, negotiations would proceed on the basis of French recognition of Algerian independence. Because the defeat of the adversary in Algeria was conceived in such broad political terms, terrorism—a political rather than a military weapon—was an appropriate strategy for combatting the colonial system. In a revolutionary context, the constructive and destructive functions of terrorism are closely related. Any increase in the FLN's control over the Algerian population isolated the French and subverted the government's authority, and destruction of the French authority structure aided the FLN in obtaining the support of the Algerian population.

Destructive or antiregime terrorism can be broken down into two categories: (1) attempts to isolate the European community as a whole (the regime, the military, and civilian colonialists) from the Algerian masses, and (2) efforts to break down the French administration and society in Algeria through the creation of pervasive insecurity. Dividing the French from the Algerian population was a way of forcing the government, the army, and European civilians to recognize the distinctness of Algerian Algeria and the inevitability of its independence. Isolation, creating the image of a beseiged government, was also a means of emphasizing this fact to the Paris government, to the metropolitan population, and to the world. The FLN wanted to disprove forever the myth of Algerian "integration" or assimilation with France and to drive the French out. No compromise was acceptable, and terrorism was used to make a moderate solution impossible for either side.

ISOLATION TERRORISM

The general heading isolation terrorism contains three identifiable subcategories of objectives: (1) cutting off police and army intelligence sources; (2) promoting general Algerian noncooperation with both the government and the European community; and (3) discouraging Europeans from making contact with the Algerian population. Only in the third case, in which the victims were Europeans, did decision-making problems arise within the FLN organization.[1] In the first two cases, isolation terrorism closely resembled terrorism aimed at enforcing the compliance of the Algerian population.

Preventing the French police and military from learning the size and movements of the rural insurgents or the urban underground organizations was a critical FLN objective, as the search for popular compliance testified. Without reliable intelligence, the French could not conduct efficient operations against ALN guerrilla bands, terrorists, or the OPA. The lack of information also encouraged blind reactions against the Algerian population, since the guilt or innocence of specific parties could not be determined; thus it was a facet of provocation terrorism.

If the French police- and military-intelligence services are regarded as indirect audiences, it seems that the FLN expected them either to accept their defeat passively, or, as a result of frustration, to engage in an active response of indiscriminate violence or the use of torture against suspects. The Algerians, however, were the direct audience; their response, a refusal to provide information whether out of fear or out of loyalty, was primary.

The FLN, in common with many other revolutionary organizations, singled out informers or potential informers as victims; apparently it frequently acted on the basis of suspicion rather than proof of complicity with the French. The victims were always individuals; thus throat cutting was relatively common. This kind of terrorism occurred throughout the war, without geographical restriction. The height of the violence probably coincided with the FLN's initial move into an area, before the organization was consolidated and its control over the population was assured. While the situation was fluid, fear was the principal means of controlling the population and preventing betrayal. After the OPA was firmly established and terrorism had intimidated those who might be tempted to inform on the FLN, indoctrination and propaganda could begin. By then the population was compromised, especially if it had failed to report the presence of the FLN or helped with sabotage. The more thorough the FLN organization and the more ideologically committed the population, the less the need to use terrorism to cut off communications. However, the instability of the Franco-ALN conflict meant that the FLN might lose and regain control of an area several times, or that an organized population might be resettled in another area. Thus the degree of FLN authority fluctuated; the organization never held "liberated areas" so firmly that the French threat was completely eliminated.

The FLN both warned potential victims of their danger and invariably claimed credit for acts against "informers." Almost every propagandistic account of their activities noted the deaths of "informers." (Claiming responsibility is, of course, a warning in itself.) This kind of terrorism also seems to have been moderately successful (although the French were able to recruit Algerian agents throughout the war). Ideology aside, terrorism to prevent Algerians from informing to the French could build on a basis of deep-seated antagonism toward the colonial power, an innate distrust of foreigners, and an unwillingness to betray one's own people.[2]

The FLN also used terrorism generally to block local cooperation with French policy in all areas and to increase polarization of opinion between Algerians and Europeans. The noncooperation campaign meant that Algerian children were forbidden to attend French schools, the indigent were forbidden to accept assistance or to work for a French employer, those in need of legal aid were forbidden to see a French attorney, the ill were forbidden to consult a French doctor or pharmacist, and peasants were forbidden to accept plots in French land-grant programs.[3] The FLN also organized collective actions such as strikes, and boycotts of French products and elections. The FLN wanted to indicate that the French had no role in Algeria. This was also an indirect form of destructive terrorism, since the French economy could not exist without Algerian labor.

In isolation terrorism, the indirect audience—the colonial elements—was the most important. The psychological responses the FLN wished to evoke from this group were discouragement and frustration, and the political response was the abandonment of efforts to "integrate" the European and Algerian societies or to implement reforms. Again, the Algerians were the direct audience; this was a large group because almost all Algerians cooperated with the French in some way. Their response was meant to be classic fear and anxiety, and a consequent refusal to deal with the French.

Because the audience group was large, including not only "pro-French" Algerians but anyone who cooperated with the colonial estab-lishment, victims were attacked both individually and in groups. The FLN threw bombs or grenades into groups of Algerian workers on French construction sites, into bars or cafes run by French but fre-quented by Algerians, and into groups of people (even children) watching films shown by the French army's Section Administrative Specialisée (SAS), a branch that had been created to perform social services and reestablish contacts with the Algerian population. FLN terrorists cut the throats of guards or night watchmen on European property. Roads leading to the polls were mined at election time. The people were forbidden to vote and risked their lives in doing so. The vulnerability of the ordinary Algerian was evidently acute because it was almost impossible to avoid contact with the French, especially when they actively promoted cooperation.

This form of terrorism occurred during the entire conflict, in both rural and urban areas, but less frequently in the metropole than in Algeria. (It would have been unrealistic and self-defeating for the FLN to forbid Algerians in France to work for the French, since their salaries served to finance the FLN's war effort.) Such attacks frequently coin-cided with elections or other French drives to encourage Algerian contacts with, or participation in, the French system. Any move by the French to break out of their isolation was countered by terrorism. As late as January 1961, while the GPRA was engaged in negotiations with the de Gaulle government, the ALN ambushed a French convoy and killed four Algerian medical and social workers (all women), a priest, and two *harkis* (Algerian soldiers in the French army).

A variant of noncooperation terrorism was directed specifically against the Algerian elite. Just as the physical acts of general noncooperation overlapped with those of general compliance terrorism, so this anti-elite activity resembled terrorism that was used to gain popular support by depriving the population of any organized indigenous leadership. It is apparent that the destruction of this elite, whether or not it was responsive to the people, removed a visible symbolic link between the colonial administration and the population. The FLN could not allow this elite to remain neutral. Therefore when it attacked prominent Algerians in the French administration, elected officials, or rural notables such as caids or gardes-champêtre, it did so both to establish control of the Algerian population and to isolate the French government.

In general, noncooperation terrorism was only a qualified success. It undoubtedly caused fear among Algerians, but it was difficult to force so many people to give up essential patterns of behavior or to resist French pressure openly. For economic or social reasons (most employers were European), because the Algerian people were caught directly between French and FLN forces, or because the FLN's threats were less credible in view of the size of the audience group, the FLN could not completely cut off relations between the two communities or between the government and the population. An indication of the FLN's effectiveness in preventing Algerians from cooperating with the French is found in the statistics showing that at the end of the war in 1962, between 200,000 and 300,000 Algerians were directly and personally "compromised" with France. Including their families, this group constituted no more than 10 percent of the total Algerian population. This figure includes 20,000 employees of the SAS, 8,500 members of "mobile-security groups" under the French Ministry of the Interior, 31,500 harkis or members of village self-defense groups, and 40,000 Algerians serving in the regular army, as well as bureaucrats and local elected officials. It is estimated that after independence between 50,000 and 60,000 Algerians were victims of retaliation because of their cooperation with the French.[4]

The FLN does not seem to have estimated the indirect audience's response accurately. Although many moderate Europeans undoubtedly grew disillusioned because of the ineffectiveness of the government's reform programs and its attempts to restore confidence, most Europeans considered fear of the FLN to be the unique motivation for the Algerian population's failure to respond to French overtures and for its participation in FLN-sponsored strikes and boycotts. This perception became an excuse for the French to wage a more determined military offensive against the FLN to free the population from terrorism. Since it could demonstrate a definite increase in acts of terrorism on the occasion of strikes or elections, the French government could prove the need for repression to its own satisfaction.[5]

An incident that may not actually have been a case of FLN terrorism but was so perceived by European opinion reveals the effect of noncooperation terrorism on the indirect audience. This was the resignation of sixty-one moderate Algerian deputies to the Algerian Assembly to protest the calling of a special session in the fall of 1955 by Soustelle to discuss an "integration" program of political reforms. Soustelle responded to the resignations by cancelling the session and abandoning his reform project. The representatives themselves publicly insisted that their action was spontaneous, but many observers believed that they had resigned under pressure of FLN terrorism since they had been subjected to a menacing propaganda campaign that also led to the resignations of many Algerian municipal officials.[6] It seems that the use of terrorism to compel noncooperation may have backfired in this case, since it led Europeans to interpret even genuine expressions of dissent as the reactions of a terrorized population.

The FLN consistently warned Algerians against cooperating with the French, and equally consistently claimed responsibility for acts of terrorism against collaborators, even when these acts caused adverse reactions from audience groups whose goodwill they sought. The false acknowledgment of the assassination of Ali Chekkal, for example, shows that the FLN leadership placed a high priority on destroying the pro-French Algerian elite.

The third form of isolation terrorism was intended to discourage Europeans from forming contacts with Algerians. It parallels terrorism aimed at halting Algerian initiatives, but in this third form, the European community, including the civil administration and the military, was a direct audience. The psychological response the FLN wanted from this group was again fear and anxiety, probably mixed with frustration and anger toward an apathetic and alien population that did nothing to protect or warn its would-be European friends. Moderate Europeans came to resent Algerian "ingratitude," especially since the victims of terrorism were often the Europeans who were the most determined to establish good Franco-Algerian relations.[7] The assassination of the administrator Maurice Dupuy, for example, had a great psychological and political effect on Soustelle's administration. In this respect, then, isolation terrorism and provocation terrorism coincided.

In this sort of noncooperation terrorism, the victims were usually individuals, as in the case of Maurice Dupuy or, in 1961, the assassination of the European director of a social center for Algerians in Oran, but there were also apparent cases of group killings. For example, in 1956, a group of French soldiers who had actively promoted a program to regain the trust of rural villages was ambushed and killed; the audience group in this case was a restricted one, however. This terrorism seems to have had no strategic significance; it was a constant but not an intensive feature of the war. To the FLN, preventing the French from winning back the Algerian population was an independent goal. Isolation terrorism aimed at Europeans seems to have been used mainly in Algeria, possibly because in France public opinion was more important, as will be seen in chapter 7.

It is difficult to estimate the overall effect of anti-European terrorism as a method of isolation or to gauge the distance between intention and result. Although the FLN probably achieved the desired psychological effect, the political response was undoubtedly less satisfactory. French officials realized that attacks on officials who were responsible for programs of cooperation were a result of the success of their overtures, and the genuinely committed people who participated in them left not because of the danger of terrorism but because of their disillusionment with French policy and their realization that such programs were often only a new guise for colonial paternalism.

An illustration of the typical official reaction to this sort of terrorism is a speech given by Resident Minister Lacoste before the National Assembly in Paris in June 1956. He explained that the aim of the French in Algeria was the liberation of its populations from terror and their rapprochement in a new Algeria, without special privileges or social injustice. To those people who believed the FLN's claim that France was engaged in a policy of extermination in Algeria, he replied that all too often they forgot the atrocities of the adversary, in particular the killings at Palestro, near Algiers. Lieutenant Artur, young and idealistic, had attempted to establish a close relationship with the Algerians in his area because "he thought that his duty as a soldier was not only to hunt rebels but to hold out a hand to the populations of Algeria." In response, he and his friends had been massacred.[8]

It is not certain that this form of terrorism was particularly successful, and it provided the French with useful propaganda. It is tempting to ascribe the discrepancy between intent and result to the difference in the identities of the direct audience groups. The FLN found it easier to influence the behavior of Algerians than to intimidate Europeans. This argument may explain why the FLN never used terrorism against European employers to force them to cease employing Algerian labor.

It is also interesting that in its communications about acts of this particular type, the FLN never distinguished between "good" and "bad" Frenchmen or admitted singling out Europeans who had aided Algerians; all of them were considered enemies. Of course, most of the victims were not civilians but members of the government or military, and the FLN never had any compunctions about attacking them.

EXPULSION OF THE FRENCH

The second major type of destructive terrorism that the FLN practiced was classic disorientation terrorism that was directed primarily against European civilians. As was previously noted, the decision to use violence against civilians was not unanimous; it was deliberately made at the top level of the FLN only after the August 1955 attacks and the Soummam Congress in the summer of 1956. In addition to destruction and endorsement, the objectives of anti-European terrorism included influencing external opinion and satisfying internal organizational needs. Its extreme utility, then, was undoubtedly a motive in the decision to use it.

Since its goal was the destruction of the French presence in Algeria, terrorism was concerned with the creation of fear, anxiety, and insecurity among all Europeans as a direct audience. The FLN, aware of the influence held by the colons over French policy, intended to make life in Algeria intolerable. A negotiated settlement would be the sole means by which the Europeans could relieve the psychological stress caused by terrorism; they would have no choice but to come to terms.

Moderate members of the FLN, including almost all the original leaders, did not want to carry this policy to the extreme of driving all Europeans out of Algeria. Subsequent FLN leaders, however, including Ben Bella and Boumedienne, were willing to take this risk. For example, the hard-line military faction opposed granting any concessions to the future European minority—even the guarantee of certain basic rights—

during the discussions that led to the Evian agreement. According to Yves Courrière, Ramdane Abane and other FLN "intellectuals" at first wanted to divide European opinion, separating the unrepentant colonialists from those who might be more flexible. The intellectuals opposed terrorism against the colons en masse because it would unite the European population against the nationalist cause and were dismayed by the August 1955 jacquerie.[9] But in the winter of 1955−1956, a European liberal effort to impose a "civil truce," promoted by Albert Camus, among others, failed dismally because of right-wing opposition. European counterterrorism in Algiers also began at the same time. In February 1956 came Guy Mollet's capitulation to the extremists in his appointment of a governor for Algeria, followed by a further surrender to ultra opinion in carrying out the executions of FLN prisoners in June 1956. According to Colonel Yves Godard, Abane "preached moderation" at this time not out of conviction but because he was too clever to use terrorism against Europeans before the establishment of a firm FLN base in Algiers.[10] This interpretation is reinforced by a 1955 FLN statement that calm was necessary in Algiers so that it could be used as a supply base for rural guerrillas, not because the FLN felt that restricting activity to the assassination of Algerian "traitors" was an efficient form of combat.[11] Although the logistical utility of Algiers may have been a factor in the FLN decision, it is understandable that the FLN leaders, many of whom were educated in the French tradition and had in the past maintained close contacts with European liberals (sometimes through the PCA), would initially hope to gain some European sympathy and would abandon this aim only when the impossibility of achieving it became obvious.

Almost any attack on Algerian Europeans, whether individual or mass-casualty, would satisfy the requirements of this form of terrorism—to demoralize and terrorize the adversary. Included in the category of disorientation terrorism were the assassinations of prominent symbols of colonialism, such as Amédée Froger, as well as the 1956−1957 bombings in Algiers.

From 1956 through the rest of the war, disorientation terrorism occurred constantly, usually in intense spells of violence. For example, in September 1959, immediately following de Gaulle's invitation to the FLN to participate in elections to decide Algeria's future, two bombs exploded in a department store in Algiers, killing 3 Europeans. A raid on a bar in a town near Algiers killed 4. Between December 1, 1959, and

January 12, 1960, 22 Europeans, most of them farmers, were killed in the Algiers region. In June 1960, a grenade was thrown into a European wedding reception in Oran, injuring 43. In August, uniformed members of the ALN fired on a crowd of European civilians on a beach at Chinoua near Algiers, killing 12 and seriously wounding 7. In September, a bus exploded in the center of Algiers. In October, the director of the *Echo d'Alger* was assassinated. In November, in the town of Boufarik, bombs exploded in a dance hall and at the nearby pharmacy where the victims went for treatment; 7 Europeans were killed and 56 wounded. In early 1961 there were several instances in which grenades were thrown into wedding receptions, soccer crowds, a group of schoolboys, buses, and other groups of European civilians. During three weeks of the unilateral cease-fire that was implemented by the French in May and June 1961, 31 European civilians were killed and 95 injured; there were 121 dead and 290 wounded among the police, army, and government officials.[12] In August 1961, an ALN unit fired on a cafe terrace in a popular European vacation spot, killing 6 and wounding 7. A grenade was thrown into a crowd on the beaches near Bône, wounding 12.

Kidnapping was one form of disorientation terrorism. Occasionally, instead of killing or wounding victims, the FLN kidnapped them, guarded them for several days or weeks, and then either killed or released them. Kidnappings followed by killings were relatively frequent during the war, with both Algerians and Europeans as victims, but the kidnapping of Europeans followed by their release was unusual. This strategy appeared to have some connection with the GPRA's emphasis on a "humanitarian" policy, which was symbolized by its adherence to the standards of the International Red Cross, mainly as an external public-relations measure. The FLN never used kidnappings as a means of obtaining specific demands, such as monetary ransoms or the release of prisoners. Its objective was apparently to create insecurity while acquiring a reputation for humanity and magnanimity and avoiding the possibility of hostile aftereffects. This strategy was used extremely sporadically.

The psychological and political responses the FLN apparently expected from the direct audience seem contradictory. It now seems plain that frustrated, fearful, and angry Europeans were more likely to reject the FLN than to accept passivity or compromise, and this raises the suspicion that disorientation was not the FLN's primary objective and that other objectives—provocation, vengeance, publicity—were more important, outweighing the adverse consequences of European hostility. The FLN analyzed the assassination of Amédée Froger, however, in terms of destruction of opposition to the revolution. He "symbolized a colonial tradition and a method inaugurated at Sétif and Guelma in 1945" and "crystallized colonialism," giving hope to Europeans who might otherwise have doubted the strength of their system. With his death, resistance to the revolution supposedly crumbled.[13] Perhaps Algerians found it as difficult to anticipate European reactions as Europeans found it to comprehend Algerian behavior. Whatever the FLN's basic intentions, it succeeded in eliciting fear coupled with anger, expressed in violent aggression and political intolerance. There seemed to be no breaking point to European hostility; it was only after the Europeans had exhausted themselves in the irrational frenzy of the OAS and incurred the enmity of the French army and authorities that they accepted what was by then inevitable and physically abandoned the struggle, most of them fleeing Algeria for the metropole.

If this was an error of miscalculation by the FLN, there were instrumental errors as well. For example, in June 1957, Yacef ordered rush-hour explosions of time bombs in three street lamps that also served as bus stops. Seven people were killed and ninety-two wounded, including some Algerians, but this was unusual; in January, the FLN had changed a planned target because Algerian employees were among the potential victims.[14] The pressure of the French paratroopers was probably responsible for Yacef's carelessness. No serious adverse effect on Algerians seems to have resulted.

The FLN's communications on its acts of disorientation terrorism were of course identical to their messages on provocation and endorsement terrorism. They publicly admitted the goal of insecurity, and claimed responsibility for European victims without hesitation. According to the FLN, the "climate of insecurity" the terrorist or *fidai* created was the basis of his importance to the revolution:

> In a classic war, the enemy is localized. There are conflict zones and rest zones. However, the terrorist helps make the national territory an immense conflict zone. There is no repose for the adversary. After hard encounters with our forces, the enemy retreats to the cities in the hope of relaxing in less perilous conditions. However, the terrorist is watching. The enemy has the right to neither calm nor forgetfulness. The Algerian army, present everywhere, strikes at every street corner.

The adversary then perceives that he must combat the entire country. Disarray, and soon defeatism, are installed in the very heart of the enemy.[15]

This excerpt gives terrorism a military air, but it is important to remember that in a revolutionary war, the enemy includes civilians as well as the military on both sides. As usual, the FLN justified its creation of "disarray and defeatism" through attacks on European civilians by references to French violence. When a reporter once asked whether, if France recognized a state of war in Algeria and treated captured FLN/ALN members as prisoners of war, the FLN would then spare European civilians, Belkacem Krim replied that since the beginning of the struggle the FLN had done everything in its power to respect the rules of war. If those rules had been broken, it was because the cruelty and blindness of the French repression had drawn the FLN beyond what it wanted.[16]

Destructive or disorientation terrorism was also specifically designed to disrupt the civilian administration of Algeria. It was intended to make government impossible by terrorizing its cadres, especially on the lower levels. This direct audience was a more restricted one than were those for the incidents of general disorientation terrorism discussed earlier. The victims, who might be European or Algerian, included postmen, policemen, and municipal employees. In this case, the victim's government role rather than his ethnic identity was the decisive factor. If the victim were Algerian, however, the act of terrorism would also serve to separate the two communities by discouraging cooperation; it might also eliminate rivals (depending on the amount of influence the victim's position carried in the government; a postman could hardly be a rival leader). The victims were individuals, because of the limited size of the pool from which they came, and they were usually killed by throat cutting or shooting. This type of terrorism was a constant feature of the war, although it was geographically restricted to Algeria.

In general terms, the response the FLN caused by its acts of disorientation terrorism was probably mixed. For example, these attacks caused military garrisons to remain on their bases and refrain from anything more than routine patrols, but they did not really deter the formation of units such as the SAS. The deficiencies of the French administration had long preceded the terrorism of the FLN. In this case, again, the FLN classified victims as "enemies" and "traitors," and there was no internal controversy over the matter.

Yet another subordinate objective of destructive terrorism was the diversion of French military and police forces from rural areas, especially when pressure on ALN guerrilla units was high. Diversion, which had probably been one function of the 1956 terrorist offensive in Algiers, also served internal FLN purposes. In form, diversion terrorism was usually urban, involving mass European casualties. It was designed to create maximum insecurity in order to occupy the government forces. According to FLN propaganda, the terrorists posed insurmountable problems for the enemy, who first had to upgrade police strength, then appeal to the military to protect urban centers. Large units were thus immobilized in the cities. In fact, the FLN explained that specific missions of diversion were sometimes planned; then a "commando, profiting from the panic caused by the action of our terrorists, can realize its objective: sabotage of an electric power station or freeing militants held . . . by the enemy police."[17] Given the massive size of the French forces in Algeria, it is doubtful that terrorism actually diverted many men from the military effort. As a factor that necessitated the very unpopular mobilization of conscripts in metropolitan France, however—that is, as a factor forcing France to commit more than her professional army—then it was successful to a certain degree.

CONCLUSIONS

To summarize, terrorism directed against the colonial system in Algeria included both efforts to isolate the European civilian community, the French government, and the army from the Algerian population and attempts to create a climate of insecurity in Algeria that would compel the enemy to come to terms with the FLN. Through the use of isolation terrorism, the FLN attempted to cut off French intelligence sources among the Algerian population, to enforce total noncooperation of Algerians with the French, and to discourage European contacts with the Algerian community. Through its use of disorientation terrorism, the second major category of destructive terrorism, the FLN aimed primarily at demoralizing and unnerving European civilians—the colonialist enemy. Its subsidiary aims included preventing effective French administration and diverting military and police from efforts to combat the rural insurgency. The polarization thus created was also intended to aid the FLN in acquiring the support of Algerians. In addition, acts of terrorism that enforced the isolation of the European community compelled Algerian compliance with FLN orders, and terrorism that was aimed at impeding European overtures to the Algerian population served the purposes of vengeance and provocation. Terrorism to discourage European initiative could also be considered to spread insecurity among the European population as a direct audience. When the terrorism that was designed to disrupt the day-to-day process of governing struck Algerians, it was again a means of enforcing both compliance and noncooperation.

In conclusion, terrorism was more effective in cutting the contacts between the Algerian and European communities than it was in destroying or driving out the French. It actually brought about a more determined French presence during the war. The European minority of Algeria would most likely have tolerated terrorism indefinitely if France had maintained a level of force sufficient to keep a minimal degree of order. Although travel, even between major cities, had to be made in convoys, farms became armed camps, and in cities the danger of bombings meant that searches, identity checks, and blockades became routine security measures, life in Algeria was tolerable for Europeans, for whom defiance in the face of danger was a part of their self-image.

The FLN seemingly was more successful in calculating the reaction of Algerians than the reaction of Europeans, whether as direct or indirect audiences. As an indirect audience to FLN terrorism against Algerians who were tied to the French, the Europeans, in whose opinion the natives were docile, childlike, and primitive, thought that the Algerian people were motivated solely by terror; consequently they ignored or overlooked the genuine attractiveness of the nationalist ideology. As a direct audience of terrorism, the Europeans were resistant to the anxiety and uncertainty that might have driven them to recognize the power of the FLN; this may have been due partly to the *macho* mentality prevalent among the *pieds noirs*, which led them to suppress fear, and partly to the fact that aggression against Algerians was a convenient outlet for their frustration and anger. The relief of frustration through aggression rather than through surrender to the terrorists was a natural response. This meant, of course, that provocation terrorism was extremely effective for the FLN.

On the whole, however, terrorism did separate the two communities, mainly because of its effectiveness in influencing the Algerian population. Each side became closed in on itself—ignorant of the other's motivations, seeing the other in stereotyped images, and communicating only with members of the same group. Both sides thus became highly susceptible to ideology and propaganda, and more amenable to extremist leadership. Mouloud Feraoun, who symbolized the ambivalence of the Algerian intellectuals who cherished French values and traditions, described the distrust and incomprehension that came to characterize Algerian-European relations. An Algerian teacher, a colleague of Feraoun's, was imprisoned by the French, and Feraoun complained that the French teachers had done nothing to help him. After his friend was released, he discovered that the French teachers had actually done everything in their power to help him. He commented:

> There are our satisfied sensitivity, our distrust without a basis, our unjust complaints! Here is how the moat is dug, how hate is fed, and crimes explained. The incomprehension, the suspicion, the lie have not finished bringing ruin down upon us. My God, what to do? Can men worthy of the name still save our country? Can all those who knew each other or who felt so close to each other, so mingled, so inseparable, who loved each other like brothers, can those people no longer make their voices heard? Will they be enclosed in one or the other of two clams separated by an abyss and from which one only leaves to die as a traitor? To fall into that atrocious abyss that is pitilessly widened by each side?[18]

Organizational Terrorism

V

Organizational terrorism is intended to fulfill internal needs of the revolutionary organization; it is inner-directed terrorism, with the FLN as the primary audience, whether direct or indirect. First, as Thomas P. Thornton has noted, terrorism may play the role of a morale builder for revolutionary militants.[1] Second, terrorism may serve to enforce discipline, control, and obedience, as it did among FLN adherents. Third, terrorism may be used as a weapon by one faction of the revolutionary organization's leadership against another; within the FLN, it was a method of gaining political influence. As a preface to this discussion, however, the issue of terrorism as a recruiting technique must be dealt with.

TERRORISM AND RECRUITMENT

Despite the contentions of many French observers of the FLN, terrorism was not a significant method of recruitment into the revolutionary organization. It accomplished this purpose only obliquely, in the sense that any terrorism that aroused enthusiasm and respect in the general Algerian population served as an advertisement for the FLN and encouraged the most sympathetic among the population to join. Terrorism that was designed to provoke French repression was also a circuitous recruiting device. The FLN's terrorism thus contributed more to the acquisition of popular support than to internal control, and it would be difficult to divide the audience group into general sympathizers and those who were persuaded to join the FLN.

Terrorism may have been used to compromise new recruits in order to bind them to the FLN, just as it was used to enlist the aid of the people in anti-French activity to compromise them with the French authorities. This use of terrorism is similar to the integrative function described by Fanon— the performance of acts of violence as a means of integrating individuals into the new revolutionary community when they have been alienated by the colonial system. The FLN is said to have ordered new recruits to perform acts of terrorism not only to prevent a change of heart, but also to test the individual's nerve and willingness. Colonel Roger Trinquier quoted a young Algerian who joined the ALN:

> From that time on I was lost, because to be admitted to the A.L.N., one first had to prove his worth; that is, to carry out an armed attack in the city. The conditions under which this was to be accomplished were explained to me. One evening, at a fixed time and an appointed place, an individual unknown to me was to give me a loaded weapon with the mission to kill the first person I came across. . . . I did what was required of me and, three days later, I entered as a member into a cell of the A.L.N.[2]

Although it is doubtful that the FLN leadership would have assigned a victim as randomly as this account suggests, an act of terrorism could have been used to test a potential recruit's loyalty. For example, when Ali la Pointe, who subsequently headed the ZAA's "shock group," was released from a French prison, he contacted FLN leaders, who suspected him of being a double agent. To test his motivation, Yacef instructed Ali to assassinate a particular European policeman, with a pistol to be given him by an unknown Algerian woman at a designated meeting place. However, as Ali discovered when he fired, the pistol was empty.[3]

It is highly unlikely that FLN leaders used terrorism directly against prospective members to frighten them into joining the organization. General Massu thought that the majority of ZAA militants acted out of conviction.[4] Recruits motivated by fear would hardly make competent or trustworthy fighters. At any rate, the FLN did not need terrorism to fill its cadres, since after 1955, when the French began putting an extensive army into the field, there was no shortage of recruits. As Germaine Tillion ironically pointed out, wherever the French army operated in strength, the FLN organization expanded.[5]

TERRORISM AND MORALE

Terrorism was useful to the FLN as a "safety valve" relieving the impatience of militants who were eager to see action against the French, or as a source of internal morale or enthusiasm. Terrorism can give the cadres of the revolutionary organization some activity to perform when the fortunes of the movement are low, and when militants are frustrated by inaction. For individuals, it is a means of participating in the revolutionary struggle, a source of personal psychological satisfaction. For revolutionary leaders, terrorism can be a means to control, and even to divert the attention of, the organization's members. It can be used to prevent spontaneous and uncontrolled violence against the enemy, as well as to thwart possible internal revolts.

The revolutionary organization is thus an indirect audience, and the victims, whether European or Algerian, are external to the movement. FLN activity in Algiers before September 1956, which consisted of assassinations of policemen and of MNA leaders, appears to have been motivated at least in part by militant impatience—that is, once the organization was created, its members had to be given something to do. Also, the FLN needed to create a diversion for the rural guerrilla forces, who were beginning to suffer seriously from the French offensive. These internal wilaya guerrillas constituted a powerful pressure group. They questioned FLN decisions that required them to bear the brunt of French repression while the political leaders of the FLN were comfortably ensconced in a peaceful Algiers. A French author reported that two CCE members told him separately that the decision to begin anti-European terrorism in Algiers was made only after much hesitation, and that the decisive argument came from the rural units, who did not understand why the CCE had refused to open an urban front. If the CCE wanted to establish or maintain its authority as head of the revolution, action in Algiers was imperative.[6] However, it is impossible to know whether or not the CCE would have undertaken the terrorist campaign that led to the Battle of Algiers if that action had not satisfied several needs simultaneously.

The ways in which terrorism was conducted against European civilians have already been described. Terrorism of this sort seemed most likely to be used when other areas of action were closed to the revolutionary movement. It is difficult to determine how successful it was in this case, but since the FLN's leaders did maintain substantial control over the organization, it probably proved to be useful.

TERRORISM AND OBEDIENCE

The second function of internal or organizational terrorism is discipline; although this objective overlaps that of morale to some extent,

it differs in that the members of the revolutionary organization constitute a direct rather than an indirect audience. In this case, terrorism
verges on punishment—a legal penalty for the transgression of an
accepted norm—and the conformist should have nothing to fear.[7]
Punishment becomes terrorism when conformity does not secure invulnerability because the limits of transgression are not clear; as E. V.
Walter concluded, "Innocence is irrelevant."[8]

The uncertainty that prevailed in the FLN organization was docu-
mented by a journalist who spent some time with ALN forces. He noted
that the least transgression or disloyalty meant death for the offender.[9]
Revolutionary movements, which lead a precarious existence, are usually intolerant of internal dissent. The outcome of their struggle for
survival depends on strict discipline and unity. Thus even the potentially disobedient are vulnerable; this is the essence of terrorism.

There is no evidence, however, that terrorism was used extensively
against the FLN organization as a direct audience to enforce obedience.
Its use was certainly sporadic and probably relatively rare. Terrorism
to secure obedience apparently occurred when the FLN was under
military pressure from the French and de Gaulle offered politically
tempting compromise solutions. For example, after de Gaulle's September 1959 offer to allow the FLN to participate in a referendum on
Algeria's future and the FLN's subsequent refusal, Si Salah, the leader of
the Algiers wilaya, informed the GPRA that 486 ALN guerrillas had
been "executed" for a counterrevolutionary plot aimed at the conclusion
of a cease-fire with the French. Si Salah apparently complained that his
units were tired, disillusioned, and eager to halt the suffering caused by
the war.[10] By 1960, French pressure had mounted and the FLN's
interior wilaya military organizations were practically nonexistent. A few
bands still roamed the countryside, but they lacked central direction,
supplies, and arms. It was at this time that de Gaulle proposed a "peace
of the brave." Now Si Salah himself decided to implement a separate truce
and was received at the Elysée by de Gaulle. In the end, his attempt to
establish a separate peace failed and an unknown amount of intra-FLN
violence followed, including his own mysterious death in an engage-
ment with French forces.[11]

A case that is on the borderline between terrorism and irrational
cruelty rather than between terrorism and punishment occurred when
French counterintelligence units provoked a series of tortures and
killings in Kabylia under the leadership of Amirouche in 1958–1959.
The French military, profiting from victory in the Battle of Algiers and

the recruitment of Algerian agents (known as *bleus* because of their blue working clothes), apparently convinced Amirouche that pro-French traitors had infiltrated the organization of the wilaya. His paranoia led to violence against the members of the organization, particularly those who had recently fled Algiers and were already distrusted by the rural guerrillas and suspected of communist sympathies. Approximately three thousand persons are said to have died in the *bleuite,* and the wilaya is said to have lost half its personnel.[12]

Despite the fact that Amirouche's policy undoubtedly created terror among the members of the Kabylia wilaya, the bleuite purges were primarily the product of a paranoid mind rather than a deliberate attempt to cause fear to accomplish a definite political purpose. Amirouche's aim was to *eliminate* all "traitors" rather than to intimidate his audience by targeting a select number of them. His violence was aberrational and totally disfunctional. Mohamed Lebjaoui describes the bleuite as

> that extraordinary enterprise of intoxication pulled off by Colonel Godard on the initiative of his subordinate Leger. On the bodies of guerrilla fighters, he slipped false documents proving that the closest lieutenants of Amirouche were spies in the service of France. Amirouche, seized with a real persecution mania, ended by having the throats cut of his most faithful companions and hundreds of young people and students who, at that time, took to the maquis to fight in the ranks of the A.L.N.[13]

TERRORISM AND INTRA-FLN RIVALRY

A third use of internal revolutionary terrorism appears to be as a tool of rivalry among the leaders of the organization. The purpose of intra-elite terrorism is to gain power within the organization and/or to influence policy decisions. The internal audience in this case is always an indirect one, but an active response is required from the direct audience, which is usually the colonial "enemy."

This form of terrorism was used by the FLN during negotiations between the GPRA and the de Gaulle government over the terms of settlement of the conflict. The issues involved in the Franco-Algerian negotiations on independence became a source of disagreement within the FLN, dividing the leaders along the lines of their political ante-cedents. As Quandt described the resulting factionalism:

> The Liberals, it seems, were most conciliatory, despite indications that de Gaulle did not feel that Abbas had sufficient authority to warrant dealing with him seriously. The Military, on the other hand, were quite intransigent, fearing that the Politicians would sacrifice at the bargaining table what they had fought for over six years to obtain, namely full and complete sovereignty over all Algeria. Barring the granting of total independence, the Military seemed willing to fight on indefinitely. More flexible than the Military were the Radicals, and to a lesser degree the Revolutionaries, who were prepared to make some concessions so long as the major demands of the FLN for territorial integrity and sov-ereignty were met.[14]

The evidence indicates that the leaders of the interior wilayas used terrorism, particularly spectacular violence against Europeans, to create a state of unrest and insecurity in Algeria that was meant to influence the negotiations. The fear and hostility of Algeria's Europeans were also meant to affect the French attitude toward the GPRA and the negotia-tions, increasing the chances of the outcome the interior leaders desired. It is difficult, however, to determine the objectives of such terrorism more precisely. Cut off from the outside, desperate for arms, the interior wilaya leaders, the ALN colonels, may have wanted simply to remind the top FLN leadership, which was no longer directly involved in the struggle on the ground, of their existence and especially of their continued suffering. They may also have intended to put pressure on the French through terrorist acts so that they would make concessions to the FLN as the only way of ending an increasingly costly involvement with an opponent who would not be permanently defeated. This purpose would combine organizational terrorism with destructive ter-rorism. Moreover, terrorism could have been a sign of the interior's intransigence and determination to continue the struggle at any sacri-fice; yet it could also be interpreted as an attempt to hasten a settlement that would end an untenable predicament for them. The French press tended to view it as a sign of intransigence. As usual, the GPRA did not deny FLN responsibility for such actions, although no public explana-tions were issued and the FLN did not explicitly claim credit. Nor were there any overt warnings. These apparently local initiatives may have been a source of embarrassment to the GPRA's politicians, but probably not to the revolutionaries and certainly not to the military faction. (It is not unreasonable to suspect the ALN general staff of encouraging terrorism to influence, if not disrupt, negotiations.) For the GPRA, terrorism in the interior may also have been a bargaining tactic of "calculated irrationality."[15] The central FLN leadership could use the threat of continued terrorism in Algeria, a factor ostensibly beyond its control, to coerce the French into making the concessions necessary to reach a settlement.

Examples showing the rather ambiguous signals presented by terrorism were relatively few; most of the factional terrorist acts occurred near the end of the conflict (which lasted almost three years). In October 1959, a conference of wilaya commanders was called in Tunis to name a new Conseil National de la Révolution Algérienne (CNRA), which would in turn appoint a new GPRA; the composition of the latter was important in light of the imminence of talks with the French.[16] The new CNRA, which was dominated by the interior colonels, was named in December; in January the CNRA appointed a new GPRA, with Ferhat Abbas again as president. Real power apparently resided, however, with Boumedienne and the general staff of the ALN. This period was marked by intense rivalry among FLN factions, and the outbreaks of terrorism in December 1959 and January 1960 can be ascribed to attempts by the interior leaders to gain influence over these deliberations. Urban terrorism against Algerian Europeans was thus used as a way of undercutting the efforts of the more moderate FLN leaders. In January 1960, the Algiers government publicly accused the GPRA of being unable to control its "ultras"; the GPRA denied this charge.[17]

There were continued indications that the GPRA did not approve, or even have advance knowledge, of terrorism against Europeans during this delicate stage of impending negotiations with the French. After the Barricades Affair, de Gaulle seized the occasion to reinforce his power by purging activists, including Jacques Soustelle, from governmental positions. The army's Fifth Bureau was dissolved, civilian authorities in Algiers regained control of police functions, and the civilian militia (the UTs) were suppressed. Apparently some FLN leaders were encouraged by these measures and by the evidence of a significant division of opinion between Algerian Europeans and metropolitan France.[18] In a speech from Tunis in early February 1960, Ferhat Abbas appealed to Europeans to cooperate with Algerians in the building of an independent nation in which all citizens would be authentic Algerians.[19] This conciliatory move coincided with another short period of intensive urban anti-European terrorism in Algeria, however, and Algerian Europeans were not particularly receptive to the idea. The general reaction was that terrorism deprived Abbas's proposals of all value and created doubt about his sincerity. Again, this might be an example of the more extremist interior military faction deliberately sabotaging the efforts of the more temperate politicians among the FLN leadership.

Another contradictory event occurred in August 1960. The GPRA announced its adherence to the Geneva Conventions on the conduct of the war, but this statement was immediately followed by the spectacular reappearance of anti-European terrorism after a lull of several months. Uniformed ALN soldiers fired on a group of Europeans on a beach at Chinoua in an area thought to be "pacified," killing twelve and seriously wounding seven.

Similar terrorist attacks occurred in January 1961, when a referendum was held on Algerian policy, and in August 1961, when a new CNRA conference replaced Abbas as president of the GPRA with Benyoussef Benkhedda, despite the opposition of the ALN and Boumedienne.

It is difficult to estimate the effectiveness of this kind of terrorism, but the FLN negotiators did hold firmly to their demands, and the French granted most of them in the Evian Accords. It is impossible to weigh the relative influence of terrorism against that of pressure from Boumedienne and the ALN's general staff. Terrorism may have lengthened the negotiation process and increased the power of the military faction, which eventually came to power in independent Algeria.

In analyzing terrorism as a facet of internal rivalry among leaders of the revolutionary movement, it is imperative to mention the death of Ramdane Abane, which resembled a terrorist assassination but was not. Despite an August 1957 reorganization of the CCE, dissension between Abane and the military "triumvirate"—ALN colonels Krim, Ben Tobbal, and Boussouf—continued. These three are generally believed to have been responsible for his rather mysterious death in May 1958. His assassination was the elimination of a specific obstacle, however, rather than an example to discourage other dissenters; for example, *El Moudjahid* announced that he had been killed in combat with the French.[20] There is also some indication that other FLN leaders were dismayed and ashamed.[21] The removal of Abane was not a typical result of internecine strife during the revolution.

CONCLUSIONS

Of the three uses of terrorism as an internal or organizational tool, terrorist activity aimed at morale building and at leadership competition affected the revolutionary organization as an indirect audience and was likely to involve the selection of European victims. These two types also outweighed terrorism to enforce obedience in sheer volume of activity. Terrorism meant for internal effect was probably less significant for the FLN, however, than any other form. Although terrorist acts were used to keep up revolutionary spirits throughout the war, terrorism for the purpose of insuring obedience and furthering intra-FLN rivalries was most common in the post-1958 period.

Terrorism is useful to stimulate and inspire revolutionary cadres or as a diversionary tactic because it is a relatively simple physical activity, the "weapon of the weak," and because its effects on the direct audience are immediate and visible. Creating fear and disruption in the enemy and thereby obtaining widespread publicity are obviously sources of psychological gratification, especially for a social group that is accustomed to being the object rather than the author of acts of violence. The likelihood that terrorism of this type will occur is probably greatest when other means of political opposition to the regime, whether violent (such as rural guerrilla warfare) or nonviolent (participation in the political system) are denied. Terrorism is a means of access to the system, a way of making an impression that maintains the enthusiasm and drive of members of the revolutionary organization who might otherwise become frustrated, impatient, or disillusioned.

Morale-building terrorism thus serves to create and to nourish revolutionary solidarity. Another means of promoting cohesion and unity is through terrorism that enforces obedience. The two functions are related to each other in the same way that endorsement and compliance terrorism aimed at the "resonant mass" are connected. Terrorism strictly for disciplinary effect appears to have been rare in the history of the FLN. Until 1958 its use was unnecessary, because once an Algerian became a member of the FLN, his choice was usually between remaining a member or risking execution by the French. There was no acceptable alternative to the FLN; the MNA was increasingly weak and discredited, and there was little incentive to join the French. De Gaulle offered a "third way," however—a respectable non-FLN path leading to independence—at a time when the FLN/ALN organization was being decimated by the French military campaign, and negotiations between the FLN and the French were dragging on without progress; in response to this threat, the FLN apparently did use some internal terrorism to combat deviationist tendencies, although its exact extent cannot be known. Competition among FLN leaders for influence over the organization's policy also resulted in terrorism in the post-1958 period. Although the audience group for both obedience terrorism and morale-building terrorism was primarily the revolutionary rank and file, the audience group for factional terrorism was the upper echelon of the FLN, particularly the GPRA. The decision makers were apparently the separate military commanders of the interior wilayas. Factional terrorism can obviously serve to undermine the credibility of moderate revolutionary leaders, making them appear untrustworthy because they are either deceitful or impotent. They are made to appear unrepresentative. Like other attacks on European or "enemy" victims, factional terrorism was a radicalizing factor that pushed the revolutionary organization toward extremism.

The Image of Terrorism

VI

The fourth function of terrorism, creating an international image, included the FLN's efforts to direct both metropolitan and foreign pressure on the French government in Paris. Involving both the colonial home country and the international environment, this particular advertising or image-building function of terrorism was a means of securing ideological support and material aid from external sources. Publicity for the movement was important as a way of influencing the audiences within Algeria, but it was also the principal means of affecting external audiences, who were physically distant from the scene of conflict and were rarely firsthand observers or potential victims.

All revolutions have possessed international implications, since related states could not afford to ignore a drastic change of regime. In modern world politics, interdependence and confrontations between East and West and North and South have heightened international sensitivity to internal change, especially violent transformations of the status quo. No civil war or revolution is purely internal. The outside world intrudes regardless of the volition of either party to the conflict. At the time of the Algerian revolution, as a result of the global anticolonial trend after World War II, independence movements had a definite moral advantage over the regimes they opposed. International receptiveness to nationalist causes increased steadily as more and more former colonies became independent states. Thus the FLN found a generally congenial international environment, and the French, especially after the advent of de Gaulle, found themselves on the side of the devils rather than the angels. The FLN was also particularly fortunate after 1956 to have newly independent Tunisia and Morocco flanking Algeria's eastern and western borders.

James N. Rosenau has suggested why internal violence is effective in attracting international attention. First, violence, much more than normal politics, has a morbid attraction for the man in the street. It excites curiosity more than any other human activity. The resulting publicity, although not necessarily a potent source of change in itself, can intensify reactions to the conflict and stimulate imitation. Second, reactions to violence tend to be amoral; the intervention of outside states in internal conflicts is thus encouraged. Third, the "explosiveness" of violence, its rapidity and uncertainty, reduces the amount of control states have over their environments. Internal violence leads to international instability because it upsets predictability and regularity of behavior.[1]

Terrorism, as a unique form of internal violence, projects an image of revolutionary strength, determination, or desperation. It dramatizes the willingness of the revolutionaries to incur high risks for the sake of a political cause and influences outside audiences' perceptions of the government and of the issue at stake. At a minimum, terrorism can discredit the incumbent government, which is compelled to acknowledge a challenge to official authority while denying the legitimacy of the revolution. Terrorism creates an embarrassing image of the incumbent's vulnerability and inability to maintain security. Robert Jervis has noted that "the image of a state can be a major factor in determining whether and how easily the state can reach its goals. A desired image . . . can often be of greater use than a significant increment of military or economic power. An undesired image can involve costs for which almost no amount of the usual kinds of power can compensate and can be a handicap almost impossible to overcome."[2] The creation of a favorable image of the revolutionary organization and an unfavorable one of the incumbent government is even more useful for an entity that does not possess the economic and military resources usually available to states. At a maximum, projecting an image of strength and of ideological correctness may inspire the most sympathetic and activist audiences to provide diplomatic or material aid—support in international conferences, money, weapons, or sanctuary.

The image created by terrorism has both international and transnational effects. The third-party audiences that are influenced by it may include the decision makers of foreign governments as well as foreign populations who are affected without the consent or control of the government. (One feature of Nasser's rise to prominence was his ability to make transnational ideological appeals to the populations of the Arab world. Terrorism can be a similar technique of persuasion.) The publicity received by terrorism is essential to transmitting the political message of the action from a revolutionary movement within one state to the citizens of another. Without the aid of the press, radio, and television, the modern revolutionary movement would find the acquisition of international recognition and support quite difficult. Terrorism thus depends on the democratic condition of freedom of the press for its success in diffusing an international image.

In the case of the FLN, the external audiences for its terrorism included the metropolitan French population as well as foreign nations. According to theories of asymmetrical conflict, the political impact on the domestic population of the metropolis of a colonial war is more important in determining the outcome of the conflict than military relationships in the field.[3] For the metropolitan population, the war is not vitally important because the future of the home country is not at stake. By transforming a distant struggle into a prominent and visible issue, terrorism can increase the political cost of the war to the colonial government.

The Soummam conference in 1956 adopted explicit goals for the FLN in relation to both the metropole and international circles. The FLN intended to disturb the economic and social life of the French people in order to force France to accept a cease-fire and to develop liberal support. It also sought the international isolation of France, the development of the insurrection in accordance with international law, and the internationalization of the issue of Algerian independence. The FLN hoped that diplomatic pressure would be applied to France, and that increased financial aid would be attracted to the FLN. In sum, from both audience groups, the FLN desired two things: first, political pressure on the French government to accede to the FLN's demand for independence; and second, direct and tangible support, whether financial, logistical, or other. In most instances, the same acts of terrorism affected the entire external environment, including the metropole, foreign states, particularly those in the United Nations, and the populations of those states. However, certain specific attempts to influence metropolitan opinion involved significant controversy over revolutionary goals; these will be dealt with separately.

TERRORISM AND WORLD OPINION

Because the terrorism that was intended to affect the external environment was identical with the terrorism that was meant to create insecurity among the European population of Algeria, satisfy Algerian demands for vengeance, provoke repression, and raise internal morale, the controversy in the FLN over the decision to attack European civilian victims was relevant to it. The fact that the mass European casualties of the August 1955 attacks in the Constantine region made world headlines was undoubtedly a consideration in the CCE's decision to begin bombings in Algiers in 1956. According to Yves Courrière, Ben M'Hidi was the primary proponent of urban terrorism, supported by Abane. Krim disagreed with the policy on the grounds that the CCE needed calm in which to work and that bombings would turn European public opinion against the FLN. Ben M'Hidi reportedly argued that European opinion was already uniformly hostile, that the FLN should instead consider Algerian public opinion, and that terrorism would serve the FLN's international goals.[4]

Another indication of an intent to influence world opinion is the timing of terrorist activity to coincide with action in the United Nations. The eight-day general strike called by the CCE in January 1957, culminating five months of anti-European terrorism in Algiers, was to be a demonstration of popular adherence to the FLN on the occasion of the first General Assembly debate on the Algerian question. It was meant to give the FLN's delegation to the U.N. "incontestable authority."[5] The threat of the strike prompted Lacoste to call in General Massu's paratroopers to crush it, and its consequent failure provoked Ben M'Hidi to order the high-casualty February 10 stadium bombings in compensation.[6] The General Assembly debate began on February 11.

The terrorism of 1956–1957 in Algiers that was meant to influence the international scene by making the revolutionary cause an issue, undermining the French position, and persuading sympathetic states (Arab or Communist) that the FLN was strong enough to deserve aid, consisted of spectacular actions. This terrorism was urban because cities are more newsworthy than the countryside and more accessible to reporters and photographers. Urban insecurity affects more people in a concentrated space than rural guerrilla warfare. The victims of violence were European civilians because casualties in this group, the dominant colonial class, were more extraordinary and more shocking than Algerian deaths. The attacks occurred in unexpected places—cafes, restaurants, stadiums, trolley cars, or stores.

Bombings resulting in numerous dead and mutilated victims were the most common method. Two died and sixty were wounded in the September 30, 1956, bombings at the popular cafes the Cafeteria and the

Milkbar. On January 26, 1957, the Cafeteria again, the Otomatic, and the Coq Hardi were bombed, leaving five dead and forty wounded. The February 10 time bombs, which exploded in crowded stadiums during soccer matches, left twenty dead and a hundred wounded. In June, explosions in lampposts killed seven and wounded ninety-two. A bomb explosion at the Casino de la Corniche on the beach resulted in eight dead and eighty-one injured. Frequently the bombs were left by young Algerian women who passed for Europeans and thus escaped the notice of security forces in European quarters.

The only assassination of an individual who was prominent enough to attract extensive publicity was the December 1957 shooting of Amédée Froger, the spokesman for European opposition to concessions to Algerian opinion. During the entire war, there were no assassinations of high-level officials in the French administration, either civilian or military. An unsuccessful attempt was made on Soustelle's life, and an effort was made in 1956 to assassinate General Raoul Salan by firing a bazooka into his office window, but the instigators of the latter attack were European right-wing extremists who found the Salan of the time too liberal for their tastes. The FLN consistently relied on bombings or other high-casualty attacks on ordinary European civilians for shock effect.

An interesting feature of the FLN's implementation of an international strategy was its deliberate avoidance of foreign victims. The international community in general was consistently an indirect audience. (It was to this standard that the metropolitan public was a short-lived exception.) The few instances of FLN terrorism that had foreign victims were undoubtedly accidental. On one occasion, an American Methodist missionary was kidnapped and released five weeks later. Any terrorism on foreign soil (Belgium, for example) was directed against the Algerian emigrant population and was not designed for international effect.

The appearance of urban terrorism followed almost two years of guerrilla warfare and implantation of an FLN organization in the Algerian countryside. When it became obvious to the FLN that the struggle between vastly unequal forces could not be decided militarily and that the traditional strategic momentum that was supposed to carry the revolution inexorably on from guerrilla warfare to full-scale conventional war was illusory, the CCE turned to spectacular terrorism—bombings and assassinations in the stronghold of the colonial elite—to restore the momentum of the revolution and attract international attention to the cause. Expanding the war into the international scene politicized and intensified the conflict.

As far as the success of this form of terrorism can be judged, it was effective in gaining international recognition for the FLN. The unexpected vigor of the French and European reaction, however, as much as the actual acts of terrorism, focused world attention on Algeria. For example, one finds the *Manchester Guardian,* the *Times* of London and the Swiss *Gazette de Lausanne* all condemning the indiscriminate collective violence against Algerians after the funeral of Amédée Froger. And it is a widely held conclusion that the crushing of the FLN organization by the French in the Battle of Algiers did more than FLN terrorism to publicize the nationalist cause. The indiscriminate arrests, the unexplained disappearances, and the use of torture in the interrogation of suspects created more sympathy for the cause of Algerian independence than anything the FLN could have done to undermine the French position, especially insofar as metropolitan opinion was concerned.[7]

It is difficult to differentiate between the effects of terrorism and the effects of the French response to terrorism, and it is impossible to distinguish the impact of the FLN's terrorism from that of its diplomatic activity, which was extensive, especially after the formation of the provisional government in 1958. The FLN's delegation to the United Nations was extremely active by means of a "corridor diplomacy," but its spokesman was reported to have explained: "You must realize that every time a bomb explodes in Algiers we are taken more seriously here."[8] The FLN also had representatives in the capitals of most Arab states. Shortly after Krim became the GPRA's minister of foreign affairs in 1960, he led an official FLN delegation that visited the Communist capitals of Moscow, Peking, Korea, and Vietnam.

On the other hand, terrorism did have certain damaging implications for the FLN. Its use allowed the French to argue convincingly that the FLN was not representative of the Algerian people but was an oppressor in its own right. Although terrorism may have been a factor in the General Assembly's decision to consider the Algerian question in 1957 (despite the French claim that the war was a purely domestic issue), it also gave French Foreign Minister Christian Pineau the opportunity to denounce the FLN as a minority trying to terrorize a majority and to link it with the Parti Communiste Algérien, which the French authorities had blamed for much of the initial FLN terrorism. Apparently Pineau's predebate speech was persuasive, and a compromise resolution was subsequently adopted.[9]

A central problem in using terrorism to influence large and disparate indirect audiences is that the spectacular violence necessary to make an impact is likely to arouse hostility. The revolutionary organization has a choice between obtaining recognition at any cost and thus risking disapproval, or seeking only sympathy. At first view, the FLN's attacks on European civilians seemed to sacrifice potential goodwill for recognition of any sort. It is evident, however, that the foreign states that would be the most horrified by these attacks (primarily those of the Western world) were unlikely to provide any support for the FLN anyway. The former colonial dependencies were less prone to resent attacks against European colonialists and more likely to provide ideological and material support. Since the newly independent states were gaining an ever stronger voice in the United Nations, the principal international forum for FLN diplomacy, it was reasonable for the FLN to focus on their response.

This decision could also be supported on psychological grounds: the reactions of neutral indirect audiences who are physically removed from the scene of violence are apt to be less intense than the emotional responses of people who are prospective victims or who observe violence personally. Distant indirect audiences, for example, the citizens of France's Western allies, probably felt curious or at least had mixed feelings. They were not likely to respond with active hostility. The fact that foreign populations had some knowledge of the FLN—at least the ability to identify it as an Algerian nationalist movement against the French—was more important to the FLN in the long run than any initial revulsion at the specific acts that brought the organization to their attention.

The FLN used propaganda to mitigate any hostile reactions to its terrorism and consistently justified anti-European terrorism in terms of French repression and vengeance. Fortunately for the FLN, French policies largely substantiated this argument. The French reaction diminished the opprobrium aroused by FLN terrorism and furnished more publicity about the struggle. The FLN, moreover, was not above denying responsibility for acts that provoked unanticipated negative reactions abroad. The mass killings at the village of Melouza in 1957, which the French exploited to discredit the FLN, prompted condemnation by all segments of opinion; even the French Left, which was normally sympathetic to the FLN, was critical. In Europe, only Radio Moscow supported the FLN. Both Frantz Fanon in Tunis and Ahmed Francis in Stockholm held press conferences to disseminate the FLN's version of the facts—that the French had deliberately staged the attack to ruin the FLN's image. Telegrams supporting this argument were sent to the pope, to Tunisia, to Morocco, to the United States, to the Soviet Union, to India, and to the U.N. secretary-general. Since the FLN did not bother to deny responsibility for attacks on Europeans, it must have considered attacks on Algerians more harmful to its international reputation.

Another example of the FLN's concern for favorable world opinion was the "humanitarian strategy," which coincided with the inauguration of the GPRA in 1958. On this occasion, and in January, April, May, and June 1959, the FLN released kidnapped Europeans with much publicity. For example, in May 1959, the FLN in Kabylia released nine military and six civilian prisoners in response to the efforts of international oganizations and foreign governments, and the GPRA issued a statement emphasizing the humanitarian nature of the act.[10] This strategy also included adherence to the provisions of the Geneva Conventions and to the standards of the International Red Cross.

TERRORISM AND METROPOLITAN FRANCE

Although metropolitan French opinion was affected by terrorism aimed at the international environment in general, the FLN also paid specific attention to this audience since its capacity to put pressure on the French government was unique and its aid to the FLN was very tangible. The "Jeanson Network" of sympathetic Europeans transported funds the FLN had collected from Algerian workers out of France to Swiss banks. Attention from the French press was also invaluable in impressing world opinion.

The decision to act directly in the colonial metropolis caused more disagreement within the FLN leadership than the decision to use terrorism against Europeans in Algeria. The CCE (and later the GPRA) clashed constantly with the FFFLN, the branch established to organize the Algerian workers in Europe. These disputes reflected a basic incompatibility in the FLN's aims of commanding the allegiance of Algerian labor, disrupting life in France, and gaining French liberal support.

During the period of the ascendancy of Ben M'Hidi and Abane within the CCE, before the Battle of Algiers, the CCE favored a French policy similar to the one that was planned for Algeria—spectacular attacks on

European civilians. In January 1957, the CCE sent Mohamed Lebjaoui to France to organize the FFFLN. He later described his instructions:

> On my departure from Algiers, the recommendations adopted by the C.C.E. concerning my mission were relatively precise. I was charged with "bringing the war home to France": that is, to carry out operations of reprisals in the French cities and countryside each time an important colonialist exaction was committed in Algeria. For each Algerian killed, a French civilian would be. The idea was simple, and evidently signified a certain state of mind. It concerned sensitizing French opinion to the reality of the war, making them understand that they were responsible for what was done in their name in Algeria and that in continuing to close their eyes, they would wind up by suffering the consequences.
> "We must have blood in the headlines of all the newspapers," Abane told me as a goodbye.[11]

However, Lebjaoui, himself a de facto member of the CCE, did not consider himself bound by these recommendations:

> Partisan of revolutionary violence, I was nevertheless, humanely as well as politically, hostile to blind attacks. The only people I proposed to aim at were several traitors and the torturers who, after their misdeeds in Algeria, came to exercise their talents here. I did not deem it any less necessary to "bring the war to France," but in a more flexible form and if possible, testifying to more imagination.[12]

Lebjaoui envisaged "several spectacular actions destined to give the French a relatively mild but very painful look at what war could be," such as knocking out the Paris subway or bus systems, making pirate radio or television broadcasts, publishing pirate newspaper editions, or flying the FLN flag from the Eiffel Tower.[13] In any case, the French police arrested Lebjaoui at the end of February and effectively annulled these ambitious projects.

After the Battle of Algiers, the death of Ben M'Hidi, and the assassination of Abane, the formation of the GPRA under Ferhat Abbas apparently led to a reversal of roles. The FFFLN, which was under the general direction of Lakhdar Ben Tobbal as GPRA minister of the interior from 1958 to 1961, demanded to "bring the war home to France," and the GPRA was reluctant. According to William Quandt, after 1957 the FLN's political elite began to recruit intellectuals who were generally only secondary leaders in Algeria but dominated the FFFLN.[14]

Apparently FFFLN influence in decision making was predominant in the fall of 1958. In September, *El Moudjahid* announced that for the first time since 1954 the FLN had decided to carry the struggle to France. The FLN had previously been content with organizational activity and efforts to combat MNA influence among the workers, as well as "execution of traitors," but this activity had had little effect on French public opinion. A campaign would be opened in 1958 to create a "psychological shock" and to provoke repression, which would demonstrate the racism of French society, generate publicity, and win sympathy for Algerians.[15] Obviously the unimplemented decision of 1957 had been forgotten.

The CCE (this was immediately before the advent of the GPRA) issued a communiqué explaining the objectives of the metropolitan strategy: (1) damaging the French war potential, and (2) carrying the same war that was being conducted in Algeria to France. The CCE also intended to reveal the "farcical" character of the scheduled referendum on the constitution of the Fifth Republic. However, the CCE did express its intention of avoiding the alienation of metropolitan opinion:

> The C.C.E. draws the attention of French public opinion to the strictly strategic character of our combat. The choice of objectives and methods shows our desire to spare civilian populations. . . . The C.C.E. from now on disengages its responsibility from attacks on civilian populations which might happen. The necessities of our struggle are imperative.[16]

The communiqué added that it was now up to the French people to abandon their indifference toward the war; by not taking a stand, they left the field free to extremist opinion and thus increased the chances of a refusal to negotiate a solution. "It is this refusal which tomorrow will cost misery and perhaps death to the population of France."[17] This combination of threat with advance denial of responsibility concluded by asking FLN militants to spare the defenseless to demonstrate the justice of their combat.

The campaign of metropolitan terrorism began on August 25, 1958, with attacks on police and civilian targets. Seven people were killed and twenty-one wounded. A police garage in Paris, a munitions factory near Paris, and an oil refinery at Mourepiane, near Marseilles, were attacked. The refinery tanks burned for several days, injuring seventeen firemen. There were more attacks on police in the following days; two French soldiers were also killed, four gasoline storage tanks in Rouen were blown up, an unsuccessful attempt was made to blow up a French battleship in the Toulon Harbor, and an unexploded time bomb was found in the Eiffel Tower. Aside from the unprecedented extent of FLN violence, the most shocking act of the offensive was the attempt on September 15 to assassinate Jacques Soustelle, who was then minister of information in charge of French television, radio, and press services in the de Gaulle government and head of the "Union for French Renewal." FLN gunmen fired on his car near the Arc de Triomphe in Paris; they were captured by the police after a gunfight in which one bystander was killed and three were wounded.

El Moudjahid claimed full credit for these acts and vastly exaggerated their importance. The journal explained that aggression in France was intended not so much to cause material damage as to create "an incontestable psychological shock, as much in France as on the international level—where the West, a French accomplice, is compelled to notice the evidence: the Algerian problem is not resolved and the referendum marks an aggravation of the war." According to the FLN, the "spectacular success" of the offensive, combined with obedience to strict guidelines respecting civilian lives and concentrating on economic objectives, had had several favorable consequences. On a strategic or tactical level, terrorism had forced France to immobilize more than eighty thousand men to guard the metropole. Moreover, the explosions at the gas and oil depots had deprived France of a day's consumption of fuel and damaged the installations for several months. On the political level, the article went on, "the myth of integration is crumbling." Racial discrimination reappeared in France; for example, the French police established a special curfew for North Africans in four departments and increased the number of arrests of suspects. "Blind and racist counter-terrorism" supposedly occurred in Lyon, Moselle, and Paris.[18]

Immediately after the opening of the campaign, Ferhat Abbas announced that although attempts to weaken the French economic and military potential would continue, instructions had been issued to avoid civilian deaths.[19] Nevertheless, the issue of civilian casualties continued to disturb the FLN. On September 22, an "Appeal to the French People" by the FFFLN reminded its readers that the FLN had intended to spare civilians and denounced terrorist attacks on civilians as colonialist provocations.[20] *El Moudjahid* simply did not admit that there were civilian victims.

On October 10, when he was again questioned on the subject of metropolitan terrorism, Abbas declared that although the FFFLN had for more than a year demanded permission to engage in anti-French terrorism, the CCE had refused until August 1958. He insisted that orders had been given to spare both civilians and police, but that orders were often disobeyed "in the heat of combat." Asked whether civilian deaths would now cease, since they were clearly forbidden, Abbas was interrupted by Krim, who broke in to say that the GPRA had not yet resolved that question.[21] A French history of the FLN also argued that the FFFLN requested authorization to explode bombs in Paris cinemas, stations, and subways but did not receive it because the FLN's central direction did not want to alienate metropolitan opinion.[22]

In any event, terrorist action ceased in France in early October—according to Yves Courrière, because the GPRA had recovered from its failure to prevent the referendum vote and had now changed to a more moderate policy, offering to negotiate without demanding French recognition of Algerian independence as a formal prerequisite.[23] This interpretation is substantiated by two different statements that were made by the FLN leadership in January and in December 1958. At the beginning of the year, the CCE reportedly insisted that terrorism was still its principal weapon. Terrorist attacks were more effective than ambushes or battles with French forces because they could not be hidden from public view. The FLN was also persuaded to return to the strategy by the fact that whenever terrorism decreased, the French announced eminent victory. Although the FLN was aware that such methods harmed its reputation with the public of France, it insisted that it did not want the support of "colonialists" but intended to achieve its aims with violence. This position was not accepted by all FLN leaders, however; by December, Krim was giving the impression that FLN leaders were no longer in favor of the type of terrorism against civilians that Abane had previously encouraged, having realized that it did not serve their cause. They now understood the influential role French and foreign public opinion could play in the solution of the conflict.[24]

The two purposes of FLN terrorism in metropolitan France were clearly contradictory. Actions designed to "bring the war home to France" and disrupt life in the metropole aroused negative responses rather than the sympathy and support the FLN desired. For example, Maurice Thorez, the head of the Parti Communiste Français (PCF), strongly condemned the action:

> The methods employed by the FLN in France have not furthered, it must be said quite sharply, the just cause of the Algerian people, which

has always benefited from the comprehension and political support of the
revolutionary French workers.

If the FLN intends to alert opinion, it is wrong. It turns opinion
against it. Far from winning sympathy, it loses it. These methods provide
too easy a case against the Algerians.[25]

Thorez concluded with what was probably the true reason for the PCF's
condemnation of terrorism: it led to official crackdowns on the Communists as well as the FLN. Probably because liberal support for the FLN
was significant in the war effort (apparently around three thousand
French were involved in the "Jeanson Network" by 1960), the FLN
finally decided to avoid antagonizing them or risking their exposure.
The GPRA had apparently agreed to the brief campaign of spectacular
terrorism in France under pressure of unexpected events—the referendum vote and de Gaulle's popularity with Algerians.

Terrorism in France thus had as its primary and direct audience the
metropolitan French population. The targets of violence were generally
material ones; victims among the police and French civilians were rare.[26]
The activity was intensely concentrated within a brief period of time. The
metropolitan offensive came at a time when the FLN's fortunes on the
battlefield were low. The Morice Line on the Algero-Tunisian frontier
had effectively cut off arms supplies to the interior, and de Gaulle's
popularity was a political threat. In retrospect, it seems that Abane's
abortive plans for 1957 were probably timed to coincide with terrorism
in Algiers and would have caused many more civilian casualties. The
1958 campaign, however, deliberately avoided the sort of terrorism that
had been practiced in Algiers.

Since the intentions of the FLN were not clear, it is difficult to
determine whether the results of terrorism were satisfactory. Certainly
there was great unease about the effects of civilian deaths. What the
central leadership wanted and what the FLN "intellectuals" wanted were
obviously two different things. The short life of the metropolitan
campaign may indicate that it was a disappointment; in view of the
relationship between metropolitan opinion and the referendum, however, the FLN's terrorism may have complicated de Gaulle's task of persuading French voters to accept his Algerian policy and thus undercut
his efforts to find a moderate compromise solution. At a minimum,
terrorism distracted the attention of the populace from the referendum
vote.

The FLN also found that its goal of winning over the Algerian workers in France and discouraging Algerian cooperation with French policy conflicted with its desire to influence metropolitan public opinion favorably. The FLN needed to control the Algerian community in Europe for financial reasons, but intra-Algerian violence had the effect of antagonizing French opinion. Since terrorism to dominate Algerians did not halt, this objective must have had priority, but the FLN did try to mitigate its adverse consequences. A common resort was blaming the MNA or the French counterintelligence services for deliberately trying to embarrass the FLN. *El Moudjahid* claimed that ·the French government "created" terrorism in France because it needed to camouflage its own crimes and because it could no longer use the "monstrous mystification" of Melouza; the revival of the MNA was France's "last card." The FLN, in contrast, remained calm and responded only by punishing traitors. "We are accustomed to being slandered but we will never again tolerate ridiculous adventurers or professional killers who try to impose their law on our people."[27]

The attitude of the FLN toward the Jewish community of Algeria (which composed approximately one-fifth of the European or non-Muslim population) can also be partially explained in terms of the metropolitan or international strategy. Some terrorism was directed against Jews as a measure of polarization—to force them to choose sides between the FLN and the French. The FLN did not consider Jews to be members of the colonial "enemy" class; seeking an alliance with liberal Europeans and Jews was also a specific objective for the conduct of the insurrection, established at the Soummam conference. Many Jewish intellectuals and professionals spontaneously sided with the nationalist cause, but terrorism was generally unsuccessful, since the commercial bourgeoisie remained loyal to Algérie française (the Jewish community left en masse along with the pieds noirs after independence).[28] The intriguing aspect of the FLN policy is the trouble FLN leaders took to deny any animosity toward Jews and to disclaim the terrorist attacks that occurred. Any hostility toward the Jewish population was vehemently denied:

> The NLF [*sic*] quickly put down the numerous provocations in this re-
> spect which were perpetrated and planned by the French authorities.
> Apart from individual punishment inflicted on police agents and counter-
> revolutionaries for crimes against an innocent population, Algeria has
> remained free from pogroms.[29]

This careful avoidance of any anti-Jewish overtones to the revolution probably reflected the FLN's desire to project an image of impartiality and fairness to its international and metropolitan audiences, as well as its goal of acquiring Jewish liberal support.

CONCLUSIONS

The FLN's objective of projecting an image abroad that would make the revolution an international issue was a significant factor in its decision to employ terrorism against European civilians in the urban and coastal areas of Algeria. The FLN was sensitive to the type of image it produced in the international community; because of its desire to achieve respectable status, it frequently used verbal and written statements to modify the effects of its violence. For example, it denied responsibility for acts of terrorism, such as the Melouza killings in 1957, that had resulted in negative perceptions of the FLN in the French metropole and abroad. The "humanitarian" strategy that included the occasional release of kidnapping victims can also be seen as an attempt to mitigate the unfavorable effects of terrorism. Moreover, the FLN commonly justified its terrorism in terms of French violence.

The desire to develop the insurrection in accordance with international law, which was expressed at the Soummam conference in 1956, was probably one reason the FLN rejected the tactic of influencing the international community as a direct audience. Nor did the FLN use terrorism as an explicit bargaining tool (for example, by kidnapping for ransom) in Algeria or France. For most of the war, it also avoided making the French population a direct audience, although the issue of French civilian victims was a matter of dispute between the central leadership and the FFFLN. The brief but intensive campaign of terrorism in France in the fall of 1958—a response to the advent of de Gaulle's Fifth Republic—produced a backlash of hostility that apparently dissuaded the FLN from further attempts of this nature. A similar result occurred when the OAS, which learned only the most superficial lessons from the FLN, tried the same tactic. If important and active support for the FLN had not existed within certain elements of the French population, there might have been less concern within the organization for the approval of this audience group. It was because nothing but hostility could be expected from the Europeans of Algeria that the FLN decided to use terrorism against them; the potential benefits in this case far exceeded any possible loss of sympathy or aid. Neutrality is permissible for foreign audiences, but not for the protagonists of the struggle, including the civilian populations. The FLN's terrorism in France during 1958 was a way of involving the French population in the conflict, but it became more important to preserve the goodwill of the French than to gain their attention at any cost. The revolutionaries were willing to incur hostility and aggression from an audience that would never furnish tangible assistance; acts of terrorism against such a group, as well as the official reaction to those acts, attracted international publicity. Such acts also served many other useful functions, such as impressing the Algerian people.

Measuring the effectiveness of this type of terrorism is a problem. It is difficult to distinguish the effects of terrorism on the FLN's international standing and reputation from those of a combination of variables, including the FLN's diplomatic and propaganda efforts and especially the violence of the French response.

The Government's Response to Terrorism

VII

The policy the regime adopts in response to terrorism is of the utmost importance to the revolutionary organization. An efficient repressive reaction may crush the insurrection at the outset, and an inefficient one may be used by the insurgents to inspire popular support. The analysis of revolutionary terrorism has shown that a revolutionary strategy of provocation of violence through terrorism can be extremely effective.

The government's response to terrorism can also be analyzed from the perspective of the incumbent regime itself; the formulation and implementation of a policy against terrorism are delicate and problematical issues for it, involving careful adherence to a middle ground between underreaction and overreaction. Policy making is rendered more difficult by certain objective features of the conflict that restrict government action but can be exploited by the revolutionary movement. Furthermore, in a colonial context, nationalism complicates the issue.

This chapter examines the French response to FLN terrorism by concentrating on three factors that are relevant to an explanation of the confrontation. First, the French government was acting within a situation in which the two sides in the conflict were distinctly unequal, and this limited the range of its choices. Second, the formulation and implementation of policy by the government were decisively influenced by weaknesses inherent in the decision-making process. Last, French policy in Algeria constituted a military more than a political response; a critical analysis of this response focuses on (1) the offensive strategy that was designed to destroy the FLN organization, and (2) the defensive strategy aimed at protecting both the Algerian and the European populations from terrorism.

THE SITUATIONAL LIMITS OF ACTION

The asymmetry or inequality of the insurgent and incumbent positions in revolutionary warfare defines the framework within which a democratic government operates. The two opponents are unequal not only in their resources and military capabilities, but also in their opportunities and potentials for political action. The government is the most handicapped politically, despite its overwhelming military superiority.

In a colonial war, one basic difference between the government's position and that of an insurgent force is that military victory is possible for the incumbent but not for the insurgent, because the latter is militarily incapable of invading the territory of the former. For the revolutionary movement, the struggle is primarily political, and the major goal is survival; for the colonial government, maintaining domination is only one among several competing policy interests, foreign and domestic.[1] The values that are at stake in the conflict are not the same for each party.

Another difference between the two sides is that the incumbent is forced to be more rigid and inflexible than the insurgent. Lucian Pye has argued that the initial government decisions are the most significant; they give the conflict structure and form, establish the parameters of action, and define the issues at stake, the character of the struggle, and the basis for its legal termination. Upholding its legitimacy must be the government's primary objective. An admission that its pre-insurrection policy was in error might damage the government's status. Thus to maintain its position the government is wedded to the status quo.[2]

A government is indeed committed and responsible to its citizens and its past record. History weighs on its decisions; admitting past faults only when confronted with insurgent violence causes a serious loss of face and requires a degree of courage and foresight that most political leaders lack. If a government grants concessions and reforms under the pressure of violence, the insurgents can claim responsibility for them and can publicly point to their achievement, which has now been given an aura of legitimacy by the government. Violence against the regime is thus condoned, and a precedent for its future use established. The regime's authority is weakened.

From the viewpoint of the incumbent, the future is mortgaged by the past, and these bonds limit the value of any promises the government may make. In the case of Algeria, the French government's past performance was an important determinant of the position it took vis-à-vis the nationalist threat. Having always insisted that Algeria was an integral part of France, the government found the concept of even a semi-independent Algeria unthinkable. The way of life of the sizable and powerful French-sponsored European elite in Algeria was at stake, making compromise difficult. A moderate solution like those reached in Tunisia and Morocco, where the settler populations were much smaller, was impossible. Furthermore, the fact that the Fourth Republic had in the past promised reforms but failed to implement them contributed to Algerian skepticism. The reform bill of 1947 had brought few changes to Algeria, and there was no guarantee that future attempts would be any more successful. The constant and callous disregard for legitimacy in the administration of Algeria, typified by the rigged elections, also lessened the government's credibility.

The insurgent, on the other hand, has only potential constituents; it is not obligated to past policies or entrenched interest groups. The revolutionary leadership is free to promise any sort of innovation; the future is largely open. The FLN could advocate land reform, political equality, and, above all, independence and the end of French domination. It could take advantage of nationalism and popular discontent.

The flexibility of the insurgents in decision making is shown in their seizure of the initiative in opening the attack on the government. An insurgent movement chooses to challenge the government's monopoly of force; without a revolutionary organization there would be no conflict. Weakness is not necessarily a deterrent because the insurgents have the option of using terrorism. A democratic regime, on the other hand, is usually prohibited from instigating open conflict against an opponent who has not yet turned to violence. One reason for this reluctance may be an unwillingness to emphasize the seriousness of the threat to government control. This does not necessarily mean that the government's past policy has not been repressive, however, in a sense provoking an insurgent response. Nevertheless, the revolutionary movement normally announces the struggle, usually through terrorism.

Paradoxically, although the insurgent can utilize extreme violence and remain relatively clandestine (although insurgents often want publicity), a democratic government cannot usually employ brutality without receiving unfavorable notice. This was particularly true of the colonial powers of the 1950s and 1960s, which were subject to the reaction of the home population as well as to international criticism. For example, knowledge of much of the FLN's terrorism against the Algerian population, which was its most significant target, did not spread beyond its audience. The terrorists, whether guerrillas or members of the FLN administrative organization, were anonymous and often indistinguishable from the civilian population. The government, however, is constantly in the spotlight, at least in the disputed territory. As Pye said, a government is by nature conspicuous,[3] especially when military forces or police move into a territory that is vastly underadministered, as Algeria was. Many Algerians in remote areas had never seen a European before the war. It is difficult for the government to conceal or deny scandals that are caused by the actions of its visible agents, and distinguishing governmental representatives is even easier when the conflict pits an indigenous insurgent against an alien colonial government. In Algeria, the FLN could deny the Melouza massacre and convince most Algerians of its sincerity, whereas the French intelligence services could not escape blame for "clandestine" counterterrorism against German arms dealers who supplied the FLN.

The use of torture in Algeria also became a controversial domestic issue in France. A historical study of the Algerian war concludes:

> France stands condemned for deeds that do not differ in degree or number from excesses perpetrated by the nationalists against the Algerian population caught between two armed camps. Yet the rebels somehow get the benefit of the doubt and tend to be forgiven for inhuman treatment. . . . Because they are or can claim to be the underdogs, they are usually forgiven their crimes by a weary national and international public opinion. The counterinsurgency forces do not fare so well because they represent perhaps another race, certainly another people and culture. . . . In a way, they must appear to be angels while fighting a dirty war.[4]

The publicity problem is critical in a society that permits a free press, but even the strictest censorship cannot stop all leaks. Modern communications media make it difficult for governments to avoid instantaneous and global publicity, and although for much insurgent terrorism advertisement is vital, the government would often prefer that its activities go unremarked.

In their legal attitudes toward the use of violence, the two opponents may also occupy different positions. Governments, which are naturally reluctant to admit that peace, security, and control of the state's territory are in danger, often deny the claim of the insurgents that a state of war exists. The regime may persist in upholding what is at best a legal fiction. On the other hand, the government may overreact to a minor threat and alarm its citizens. Pye noted that "governments generally find it difficult to avoid giving a highly legalistic definition to most insurgency conflicts," seeing them as threats to law and order, on the same scale as riots and mass demonstrations.[5] "The manner in which a conflict is defined in the beginning is also likely to affect the entire course of an insurrection, because it places certain definite limits upon the ways in which an insurrection can terminate."[6] The proponents of "law and order" usually insist that the government cannot negotiate with the revolutionary movement and are willing to accept only a complete surrender, thereby prolonging and heightening the confrontation.

A related problem, which Pye considered fundamental, involves the way the government treats individual insurgents—whether as outlaws and common criminals or as prisoners of war. The legalistic position dictates that insurgents are bandits and common criminals; the government does not want to dignify them by allowing them the status of enemy soldiers. A legalistic refusal to reward defections makes it difficult for the government to implement any sort of convincing psychological warfare, however, or to persuade its opponents to surrender and rejoin the political system. Once a government has chosen the hard-line view, it may be forced to back down from firmness to leniency in mid-conflict, with a consequent loss of prestige.[7] The refusal to treat captured insurgents with the clemency that would be accorded prisoners of war encourages the use of harsh interrogation methods, since the insurgent has no other incentive to confess. The French government enforced the death penalty against all convicted members of the FLN, and torture during interrogations was standard operating procedure. The only alternative for the FLN prisoner was active participation in the regime's anti-insurgency program, and this was available only to a few. This form of polarization works against the government in the long run, especially when it prompts the population to demand terrorism in revenge.

In the French case, two different incumbent regimes must be considered. The Fourth Republic tended to take a legalistic view of the conflict, and the successive governments from November 1954 to May

1958 publicly refused to deal with an adversary they considered an outlaw. However, the willingness of the Mollet government to undertake secret negotiations with FLN representatives in 1956 probably reflected a desire to back away from the official no-concessions policy. The army overthrew the government in May 1958 because the Pflimlin cabinet was rumored to favor negotiations. The Fourth Republic had very little leeway in its ability to disown the policies of preceding governments in Algeria, however, since the same politicians and parties had composed a continuing series of governments; the political game of musical chairs limited the government's options. Yet by basically agreeing with the FLN that reforms were essential and then failing to impose them, the Fourth Republic lost authority with Algerians. The policy of treating FLN prisoners as criminals and the use of capital punishment and torture, frequently based on dubious evidence, provoked Algerian resentment while they encouraged dangerous European illusions of a permanent French "presence."

It was somewhat simpler for de Gaulle to renounce the past, but even the Fifth Republic was bound by the policies and the politicians of the Fourth Republic, as well as by the military and the right-wing pressure groups that had helped de Gaulle rise to power. Nonetheless de Gaulle made a visible effort to escape the legalistic definition of the conflict and to redefine its terms in a more flexible manner. He offered to negotiate with the FLN and to allow it to participate in honest elections on Algeria's future. Executions of FLN prisoners were temporarily halted. The arrangement of a mutual cease-fire was attempted, and when that failed, de Gaulle decreed a unilateral truce, although military opposition to this policy made its implementation uncertain.

De Gaulle's efforts to reach a compromise were also hampered by other factors, particularly the growing intransigence of the FLN. The established pattern dictated that only full surrender could end the conflict. Ironically, the leaders of the Fourth Republic did not realize that by insisting on a zero-sum game, they were setting the stage for an eventual French defeat. When the government altered its course and became willing to compromise, it was too late to change the stakes of the game. De Gaulle's efforts to find a middle ground between the positions of *Algérie française* and *Algérie algérienne* were doomed to failure.

Another asymmetrical aspect of revolutionary war is that the insurgents' aim is to promote disorder, but the incumbent must maintain order. Restoring order is a practical necessity, but it is complex and costly, especially compared with the ease with which the insurgents can cause disorder. The cost of terrorism is much lower than the cost of its prevention. David Galula emphasized this point: "disorder—the normal state of nature—is cheap to create and very costly to prevent."[8] Since the government must accept the responsibility for maintaining order, its costs must be much higher than those of the revolutionary organization. For example, Galula mentions that in Algeria the FLN budget at its peak was only forty million dollars per year—less than the French spent in two weeks. According to Galula, however, this disparity does not increase in proportion to the amount of disorder; the government can handle an increase in insurgent disorder without additional expense after the disorder reaches a certain point—the point at which the law of diminishing returns begins to operate for each side alike.[9]

The government's efforts to cope with disorder are costly in terms of manpower and resources, and its measures designed to restore order, particularly in response to terrorism, are themselves disruptive; they disorient the population, create insecurity and anxiety, and thus serve the purposes of the insurgents. Security measures involving repression, especially against the dominated masses, further aid the insurgents by alienating the population. Attempts to restore order are to a certain degree self-defeating unless the population is convinced that they represent an essential safeguard against a clear terrorist danger.

Another unequal factor in the conflict is the role of popular apathy; it harms the government because popular loyalty and allegiance are fundamental attributes of the incumbent's station. A population that refuses to choose sides is less damaging to the insurgents, since popular support and legitimacy are goals rather than requirements of their position. A lack of popular sympathy may hurt the insurgents as the conflict progresses, but initially they have nothing to lose and everything to gain, whereas the opposite is true for the regime. The fact that control of the population of a state is at stake in the conflict demonstrates that the government has somehow failed.

DETERMINANTS OF THE RESPONSE

Many determinants of governmental policy are extrinsic to the strategic relationship between the two adversaries in the conflict. First, the internal decision-making capabilities of the political system influence the government's attitudes and actions. Second, pressures from the outside political environment help to determine policy. In the case of Algeria, this environment included the European settlers of Algeria, metropolitan French public opinion, international opinion, and last but not least, the French military establishment, which, despite its formal status as an instrument of government policy, functioned as an independent decision-making body, an agency with a political will of its own. Because of the Fourth Republic's weakness and its tendency to regard the response to terrorism as a police or military problem, the French army gained considerable power.

In examining these determinants of Algerian policy, it is naturally essential to distinguish between the Fourth and Fifth Republics. It is not, however, necessary to differentiate the six governments of the Fourth Republic during the Algerian revolution, since policy changed only incrementally from one cabinet to the next.[10]

In terms of capability for action, the Fourth Republic was notoriously weak. The structure of the government was weighted toward a parliament that united only in opposition. As Philip M. Williams described the problem of Algerian policy, "there was a majority neither for victory at any price nor for peace by negotiation, but only for ineffective compromise solutions. . . ."[11] Because the Mendès-France government had dared to act decisively, the National Assembly reversed it in February 1955, and thus issued a clear warning to future prime ministers who might be tempted to show such boldness. Initiative was only a catalyst that crystallized opposition. The safest method of remaining in power was to avoid making any enemies, therefore to avoid commitments. The inner-directed political game operated by periodically reshuffling the same men among different posts. The government followed a cautious path and never seriously attempted to lead its constituency; thus it was vulnerable to outside pressure, especially from the organized parliamentary lobbies. The means that were at the government's disposal for implementing policies in Algeria were limited, so that even when a position was finally formulated in Paris, there was no assurance that it would be effected in Algeria. This impotence and uncertainty severely reduced the regime's credibility. The 1947 reforms remained a dead letter, but no one in Paris particularly minded this state of affairs before the 1954 outbreak brought the urgency of the situation to their attention. Algeria's problems were far away, and national politicians were mostly content to accept the recommendations of the Algerian colon lobby.

The colonial interests in Algeria were the oldest and strongest pressure group on the scene. This lobby traditionally shaped national policy toward Algeria, which focused on the maintenance of French domination. Most settlers, rich colons or average pieds noirs, were unable to see that the structure of colonialism in Algeria had become an anachronism, and that in the long run the metropole would not consent to the burden of indefinitely holding Algeria by force. They failed to see that although the overall underdevelopment of Algeria was remunerative for them in the short run, it would become a handicap when Algeria's financial cost to the metropole became prohibitive. Since the bulk of the French army was conscripted in the metropole, Algerian Europeans were almost totally dependent on France for defense, and in the end, this economic and military dependence was a factor in ruling out a Rhodesian-type solution. The vested interests in Algeria thought that repression discouraged nationalist agitation, but it was actually a catalyst to violence. For the majority of Algerian Europeans, the only conceivable position was to meet force with force and to hold the lid on rising Algerian demands for improvement in their status. The colons' perhaps realistic fear of being "abandoned" by France became paranoiac, but it did not induce them to take a sharper look at the future. Led by extremists, the European population reacted to all suggestions of reform, which might have persuaded the metropole to sacrifice more on the behalf of Algérie française, with violence against Algerians and against the Paris government. FLN terrorism was a factor in pushing them to intransigence and to the refusal to compromise that eventually brought about their destruction.

The power of the ultra Algérie française lobby was augmented by the support of much of the French military establishment. Specific examples of extremist influence on Paris-made policy are numerous, including the organization of European civilians into armed self-protection groups and the imposition of the death penalty against FLN prisoners. Most significant was Prime Minister Guy Mollet's rescindment in 1956 of his nomination of General Catroux as governor-general of Algeria after riots in Algiers.

The metropolitan population did not initially take a strong interest in the affairs of Algeria. The French people saw the conflict as a case of preservation of an impersonally conceived national honor; they found it especially necessary to maintain control in Algeria after the humiliation of Indochina, but they were not vitally concerned. The only metropolitan lives and futures that were directly and constantly threatened were those of the men who were in military service, and as more and more conscripts were sent to Algeria, popular discontent swelled. The voters of the French metropole were generally more liberal than those residing in Algeria. The Mollet government of 1956 was elected on a reform-and-peace program, and successive cabinets were pledged to a superficially liberal policy: reforms plus "pacification." The gap between popular expectations of reform and a settlement, which were encouraged by the good intentions of the Paris government, and the actual policy that was carried out in Algeria created frustration and unease. Politicians of the Left and Right exploited and deepened popular divisions.

International opinion also had a certain influence on the government's decisions. For example, the fear of provoking an unfavorable United Nations vote on the Algerian question was one of the reasons the Fourth Republic was eager to pose as a reformist administration. In March 1957, Mollet issued a "declaration of intentions" that referred to his government's secret contacts with the FLN and blamed the continuation of the conflict on the FLN's intransigence.[12] Another example of foreign influence was Senator John F. Kennedy's well-publicized pro-independence stand on Algeria. In 1957, Kennedy introduced a resolution calling for the use of American influence to encourage France to recognize Algerian independence. This action provoked a bitter response from Governor-General Lacoste, who thus attracted more publicity. The FLN representative at the United Nations reportedly provided Kennedy with the factual background for his speech. Kennedy's position on Algeria naturally bore more weight in France when he became president in 1961.[13]

The distracted and debilitated Fourth Republic was overwhelmed with immediate domestic pressures, however, and its consequent neglect of international affairs included allowing the army and the administration in Algiers to alienate newly independent Tunisia and Morocco by hijacking the airplane carrying the FLN's "external delegation" from Rabat to Tunis. Bourguiba's increased Tunisian aid to the FLN was a direct result of this lapse of French authority.

The most important single influence on daily policy was the military establishment. Unable to control the situation, the government voluntarily left the task of combatting FLN terrorism to the army. Ultra European calls for stronger measures occasionally had direct consequences, such as the executions of FLN terrorists and the arming of European civilians, but these were moves the army approved. Although it was not a monolithic bloc, the army was sufficiently organized to make and implement decisions. The power of the military increased after 1956, when the officers of the professional army arrived in Algeria from Indochina.

The subject of the French army's conduct during the Algerian war is a complicated one, which several competent authors have treated in detail.[14] The segment of the professional army that was most powerful in determining Algerian policy espoused the theory of *guerre révolutionnaire*, which underlay the army's response to FLN terrorism. The *guerre-révolutionnaire* theorists understood that control of the civilian population was the major aim of the insurgents, but they incorrectly estimated the means by which this was to be achieved. According to this doctrine, "psychological warfare" was merely a technique, one that was simple to master and necessarily more effective in the hands of a superior ideology—that of Western Christianity rather than the atheistic Communism that was behind all revolution. "The world of revolutionary war was largely one in which skilful manipulators could turn the masses in any chosen direction—if only the manipulators' skills were great enough."[15] No indigenous revolution was possible; all internal wars were actually forms of international Communist subversion. A French officer declared, for example, that "Algerian nationalism was an artificial dialectical creation" of international Communism.[16] This miscalculation of the power of the nationalist ideology, especially compared with the slight drawing power of the promise of "integration," was carried to its logical extreme in the insistence of the proponents of *guerre révolutionnaire* that if the FLN's parallel government, the OPA, which supposedly maintained itself solely through terrorism and psychological manipulation, could be destroyed, then the entire rebellion would collapse.[17] These theorists saw no valid connection between the actual conditions of Algerian society and politics, which they recognized to be unjust, and the motives of the FLN. To them, reforms would be useless in quelling the insurrection, since its causes were not indigenous.[18]

In addition to being an emotionally and intellectually satisfying answer to a complex problem, the doctrine of revolutionary warfare was a means of protecting the army's vested interest in conflict. The admission

that political reforms and negotiations could serve a constructive purpose implied that the army's role in Algeria was not essential and
removed the justification for the use of violence against the FLN. Such
theories were a means of self-defense against feelings of uselessness and
humiliation that assailed the French after the Indochina debacle.

The exponents of *guerre-révolutionnaire* theories developed specific
explanations for the strategic uses of terrorism in an insurrection.
According to them, the first phase of terrorism is aimless and spectacular;
in it the terrorists simply seek publicity and attention for their cause. The
next stage is more selective; it is aimed primarily at eliminating "traitors"
to the rebel cause. In the course of this phase, systematic terrorism is
combined with propaganda and psychological indoctrination of the
masses. The population refuses to communicate with the government
for fear of reprisals. The victims of terrorism include any individuals
who are capable of persuading the population to accept the established
order; they are selected as representative examples of chosen groups of
people. Neutrals are forced to choose sides. Terrorism is also used to
provoke the regime to repression. Only after these two phases of
terrorist activity, according to the theory, do the rebels move to guerrilla
warfare, the establishment of parallel government structures, and then
conventional warfare.[19]

Although this argument showed some understanding of the process of
terrorism, it failed to perceive that in Algeria, revolutionary violence was
accompanied by the powerful ideology of nationalism, by anti-French
xenophobia, and by considerable organizational effort on the part of the
FLN. It did not detect the range and complexity of terrorism, especially
its functions in avenging victims of French violence and creating
enthusiasm among the supporters of the FLN. The French military
gained the mistaken impression that "intoxication" of the masses and
fear were the keys to control. This view of revolutionary warfare was also
misleading in its assumption of an inevitable progression from terrorism
through guerrilla activity to conventional war. When the army held the
FLN to the first two stages, it thought victory was complete; this caused a
feeling of betrayal when the de Gaulle government proposed a negotiated solution. The army saw terrorism only as a precondition of the real
war it was equipped to fight.

Some French military theorists also condescendingly assumed that
terrorism was a product of the barbarity of the Arab character or of the
Islamic faith. For example, one writer claimed that the rebellion was a

djihad, or Muslim holy war, and therefore not motivated by political or social grievances.[20] Another military thinker declared that the FLN's taste for violence was imputable to the "Arab style" rather than to Islam. In his opinion, the fact that men as well informed and as attentive to international opinion as certain of the FLN leaders failed to perceive that their excesses had self-defeating international effects indicated that FLN terrorism was not "methodical" but was the result of a specifically Arab seal on the "good revolutionary use of violence."[21] This statement is particularly interesting in light of the fact that French violence was more self-defeating in terms of international effect than FLN violence. The same analysis also noted a certain spiritual impotence or sterility among Muslims that was properly Islamic or Arab and that made it difficult for the FLN to move beyond negation and destruction. To Muslims, it went on, violence became sacred and led to excesses of terrorism that were serious political errors—that is, ethical considerations aside, all methods of subversion depend on a necessary amount of terrorism at certain moments, but an excess of violence constitutes a tactical fault.[22] Another view, one that was prevalent in military circles, was that FLN terrorists were drugged before committing acts of terrorism.[23] This charge lacked any substantive basis and ignored the well-known fact that the FLN strictly forbade the use of alcohol or drugs.

Colonel Roger Trinquier, an advocate of *guerre-révolutionnaire* doctrines and a specialist in the organization of populations, has devoted much attention to the problem of terrorism. His prolific writings give the reader the impression that Trinquier envied the terrorists' mobility and power. He tended to exaggerate the value of terrorism as the principal weapon of insurrection: "We know that the *sine qua non* of victory in *modern warfare* is the unconditional support of a population. . . . If it doesn't exist, it must be secured by every possible means, the most effective of which is *terrorism.*"[24] Trinquier contended that "psychological action" was only effective in peacetime, and that French psychological action failed in Algeria because terrorism was not suppressed first. A population had to possess at least "the illusion of freedom" to be psychologically manipulated.[25]

To combat terrorism, Trinquier thought that martial law should be declared and that the army should institute a methodical program of population control. Every village should have its military garrison, and the army should arrest, interrogate, and imprison all members of banned political parties. Anyone who was guilty of complicity with the terrorists should go before a military court. The population should be strictly guarded and controlled: no movement or transportation without special passes, all strangers subject to arrest, and a curfew. The military should evacuate all isolated farms and destroy the buildings. Farm workers should be subject to rigid controls, and anyone attempting to run away when summoned should be shot. If these measures were enforced, the population would feel confident and would aid the army, and then psychological action would become effective. Colonel Trinquier feared, however, that a democratic regime would not take these steps in time.[26] This is fortunately so, but it is also doubtful that the immediate application of the authoritarian measures he described would engender confidence. Similar programs that were used in Algeria protected Europeans but antagonized Algerians. Trinquier also overlooked the fact that these security operations would be exorbitantly expensive in terms of resources and manpower, as well as disruptive to both economy and society.

The military interpretation of terrorism explains in part the inevitable failure of the French army's response to the FLN. The army's conception of terrorism was limited to its purely physical or violent aspects; it completely ignored or misunderstood the psychological and political implications, and the civilian authorities did not correct this impression.

The military attitude toward insurrection also had profound political implications for the relationship between the army and the Paris government. The army was convinced that the government had called it in too late, after the terrorist movement had gained effective control of the Algerian population, and that the politicians in Paris were not willing to apply the firmness that was needed to defeat the insurrection. Such complaints may seem ironic in view of the Fourth Republic's general subservience to military demands, but the army blamed a scapegoat civilian regime to excuse deeper failures. Military bitterness culminated in the May 1958 overthrow of the Fourth Republic and the installation of a de Gaulle government. After that, hostility seemed to decline as the number of *guerre-révolutionnaire* adherents who were willing to revolt against the Fifth Republic so that they could remain faithful to their conception of warfare and to absolute victory in Algeria decreased.

A splintering of the French army that became significant after 1958 also had an effect on the combat against the FLN. Professional army units—paratroopers and other elite intervention troops that had been influenced by their experience in Indochina—were the most politicized elements in the military. The theory of *guerre révolutionnaire* was firmly implanted among these troops, who had the more glamorous and dramatic combat assignments. The "paras" had their rear bases in the Algiers area, where they formed contacts with civilian ultras. The French government turned the fight against terrorism over to these forces, and the frustration of having to do this dirty "police work" was one reason for their dissatisfaction with the politicians who had gotten them into the mess but would not pursue victory at any cost.

Yet not all the professional army was seduced by the doctrine of *guerre révolutionnaire*. Some members of the military officer corps, weary of stalemated colonial wars, were eager to get on with the business of making France a significant Western military power, particularly with the development of the *force de frappe* and a modern mechanized army. It was to this group that General de Gaulle himself, a longtime advocate of an *armée de metier*, belonged.

On the other hand, the conscript army, which was made up of inexperienced, young enlisted men, led a much duller and much more routine life than either element of the professional military. Isolated in the countryside, dealing with a suspicious and alien native population on a daily basis, they were unenthusiastic about the war and eager only to go home. It was to this dispirited group that de Gaulle could appeal in his power struggles with the rebels in the professional army.

The influence of the *guerre-révolutionnaire* elite on Algerian policy was strongest from 1956 until 1958, when it reached a peak; after that it began a slow decline in response to the increase in de Gaulle's power. Having helped to overthrow the Fourth Republic and establish the Fifth, the would-be kingmakers were dismayed to learn that de Gaulle did not share their doctrines and did not intend to act as the army's instrument in Algerian policy. De Gaulle was determined to escape the policy framework that had been established under the Fourth Republic. As much as possible, he resisted yielding to traditional interest groups on Algerian policy. He was extremely wary of conservative pressures on governmental representatives in Algeria. He apparently felt little sympathy for the Europeans of Algeria and began cautiously to oust military officials from the positions of civilian responsibility they had assumed after May 1958. He improved the decision-making capabilities of the French political system with a new constitution that weighted the Fifth Republic on the side of the executive branch rather than the legislature. De Gaulle possessed exceptional leadership qualities and took sole charge of Algerian policy. He also profited from a growing war weariness among the metropolitan French population, who began to think that preservation of the national honor was not worth the expense of maintaining a colonial empire.

French military strategy, especially the sealing off of the Algero-Tunisian frontier, succeeded in containing the FLN's conventional and guerrilla warfare within tolerable limits. Through the use of terrorism, excellent organization, and ideological appeal, however, the FLN was able to mobilize the Algerian population. Because the FLN had this base of support, and because terrorism requires minimal resources, the army could not entirely eliminate FLN violence without unacceptably high cost. Even to restrict the FLN to sporadic terrorism, France would have had to station large numbers of troops permanently in Algeria. In addition, the violence of the OAS in France and Algeria destroyed what remnants of sympathy the metropolitan population might have felt for the colons. The political and economic burden of maintaining the French "presence" in Algeria was too heavy to pay, especially in light of de Gaulle's sensitivity to international opinion and his foreign-policy ambitions. His aim of establishing cordial relations with the nonaligned and developing nations and his preoccupation with the force de frappe precluded the continuation of a colonial war in Algeria.

OFFENSIVE AND DEFENSIVE STRATEGIES

Since the Fourth Republic, through choice, and the Fifth, through constraint, had left the major response to terrorism in military hands, the entire period 1954–1962 was characterized by unity of action and motivation. The two principal military strategies against terrorism can be logically divided into offensive and defensive methods. A defensive strategy consists of protecting the civilian population from terrorist attack—that is, depriving the insurgents of their victims and consequently their audience. An offensive strategy is aimed at eliminating the threat of terrorism by destroying the terrorist organization.

The regime's main problem in combatting terrorism is protecting the population from violence without creating undue disruption and hardship. Security measures necessarily involve actions that upset normal life patterns, but the population will probably accept a reasonable amount of interference if it is demonstrably effective against terrorism. When the terrorists are an indistinguishable part of the population to be protected, however, a number of problems arise. In Algeria, protection of the European population, for whom the FLN was the visible enemy, was reasonably effective; protection of the Algerian people, who were a much more vulnerable and significant audience for FLN terrorism, failed.

Europeans were easier to protect since they were fewer in number, and were easily differentiated from the FLN (in most cases). The army often stationed permanent garrisons at large farms in rural areas and in almost all European towns or villages after 1955. In urban areas, the military blocked off Algerian quarters from the rest of the city and controlled movement into the European sectors and into and out of the city. The methods were disturbing, but they irritated the Algerians, who were always stopped for identity checks and searches, far more than the Europeans, who were generally exempt unless they were known to be members of the PCA or openly "liberal." The FLN terrorists exploited this racial discrimination to their advantage by choosing attractive Algerian girls who resembled Europeans to plant bombs in European quarters.

Another way of insuring the safety of Europeans, both urban and rural, was to organize them and provide them with the means of self-defense. The government was at first reluctant to arm European civilians, rightly fearing that it would be difficult to control them, but the Europeans blamed the August 1955 massacres of Europeans by the FLN in the Constantinois area on governmental failure to arm civilians. As one author explained, from 1956 on, after the government had surrendered to these demands, "normal politics in Algeria were suspended."[27] The arming of untrained and undisciplined Europeans was a crucial French policy error. The paramilitary Territorial Units were responsible for extensive and indiscriminate violence against the Muslim population; their efficiency against FLN terrorism was limited, and they undoubtedly provoked more violence than they prevented. European paramilitary activity directly contributed to political instability in France and Algeria; FLN terrorism stimulated European pressure, which led to the official policy of arming civilians, who became a threat to any potentially moderate and flexible regime. European aggression against Algerians obstructed a reconciliation of the two communities; the integration of Algerians into a reformed political system may have been a vain hope anyway by 1956, but European violence did aid the FLN, for whom compromise was also anathema.

French protection of the Algerian population ranged from poor to nonexistent, especially in rural areas where the FLN organization usually went unchallenged. The French army did not possess sufficient troops to protect every village and hamlet in Algeria's vast and rugged territory, which was traditionally underadministered. Even the most thorough coverage or *quadrillage* could not establish permanent garrisons everywhere Algerians were concentrated,[28] and the enormous spaces and difficult terrain made patrols inefficient. The French soldiers who were charged with garrison duty were usually short-term conscripts who were ignorant of local customs and language. Under a constant threat of terrorism themselves, they were understandably reluctant to risk their lives in the service of "pacification," and were powerless or unwilling to combat clandestine FLN violence against Algerians. Many garrisons sent out armed patrols during the day but remained in fortified camps at night, leaving the field free for the FLN.[29] Although successive military leaders tried to remedy these defects, it was difficult to convince drafted soldiers that the risks a more active French presence would entail were worth it. In addition, many upper-level officers were more interested in glamorous large-scale operations, which earned promotions and decorations, than in day-to-day, unspectacular, unheroic protection of Algerian "natives."

The Algerians resented French indifference. Mouloud Feraoun's journal mentioned an incident that occurred in September 1956:

> Day before yesterday someone fired on the *amin* of Ikh here . . . at 7 p.m. They wounded him slightly. That didn't bother anybody. Yesterday, they fired on a captain. After having slain the terrorist who was unable to escape, the soldiers patrolled all day, rounded up Kabyles, searched everywhere. A petty official told me: You see what they do when it concerns one of them (them, the French): they move heaven and earth, they kill one suspect and imprison others. Perhaps the suspect is really guilty. Just so they stop there! When it concerned the *amin*, nobody was upset. In sum, the French want us to exterminate each other mutually.[30]

The French attempted to set up local Algerian self-defense programs on a limited scale, but these policies, along with plans to use Algerian troops (harkis), were neither productive nor widespread. Providing Algerians with arms to use against the FLN was a delicate affair, requiring close and informed supervision. It is possible that carefully structured, controlled, and extensive arming of villages might have produced more impressive results, but by the end of the war, the army claimed only 1,840 villages as part of a self-defense system; one scholar estimated that this was only two-thirds to three-quarters the number necessary to maintain security in the Algerian countryside, and that it was only useful as a temporary measure anyway.[31] Much self-defense work was done towards the end of the war rather than earlier, when it was most needed.

Much of the French effort to protect the Algerians from terrorism fell under the aegis of the "psychological-action" services, which relied on population control, especially regroupment. Whether the real motive for the resettlement of populations was to protect them from terrorism or to clear the terrain for military operations against guerrilla bands is debatable. At least one million Algerians were settled in camps administered by the military before June 1961, and many more were simply uprooted without provision for resettlement.[32] The results of French policy have been described as a "veritable diaspora," "an upheaval without precedent in the history of Algeria." French authorities imposed artificial arrangements, discipline, and order that destroyed the traditional social structure and civilization, uprooting peasants from their lands and reducing them to idleness and unemployment. The resettled inhabitants' resentment of their enforced and permanent inactivity and their abrupt displacement into desolate French-style villages or urban shantytowns "dominated the whole of their existence."[33] Programs of regroupment as well as *quadrillage* encountered the same problem: despite the presence of fortifications and guards, the French could not prevent clandestine FLN penetration of regouped populations who had been made much more susceptible to nationalism by their experience:

> Groups of different origins were brought together, a fact which tended to weaken the old communal ties. A new type of solidarity now made its appearance, quite different from the former solidarity and closely linked to a feeling of revolt against commonly shared conditions. The real and sometimes terrible material misery they had to endure was, however, nothing compared to the moral misery of these men who had been torn from their familiar world, their home, their lands, their customs, their beliefs, everything that helped them to live.[34]

According to another observer, "a more favorable ground for subversion could hardly be imagined than the resettlement centers, with the concentrated hatred and frustration of thousands."[35]

A less destructive means of substituting French for FLN control of the population was the creation of special military administrative units, the SAS and SAU (Section Administrative Spécialisée and Section Administrative Urbaine), which attempted to remedy the political underadministration of Algeria and to provide much-needed social services. The ultimate purpose of these organizations, of course, was to gain support for the French cause, but the effort lacked coordination, and there was little sympathy between the SAS-SAU—controlled by the civilian administration and staffed by conscripts—and the combat commanders. Brutalities committed during a day's operations by elite combat-intervention troops seeking military victories and high body counts could erase the results of months of conciliatory work. Moreover, not all SAS-SAU officers were dedicated to improving the lot of the Muslims, and there were no uniform standards for their training or education.

Although administrative penetration into the Algerian countryside was a necessity from the French point of view, the drawbacks of the plan were numerous. They included: (1) the limited scale of the program and the lack of funds; (2) the absence of centralized control and support from the top-echelon military establishment; and (3) the fact that the French were inescapably alien and frequently "paternalistic" in their attitudes toward the Algerian people.[36] The involuntary association of the SAS-SAU with the repressive apparatus of the French army compromised even their best-intentioned efforts.

In general, the French army failed seriously in the task of providing protection against terrorism for the Algerian masses. Under such circumstances, it was futile to ask Algerians to commit themselves to the cause of France. It was evident by 1958 that polarization of opinion would work against rather than for the French, since most Algerians chose the FLN whey they were forced to take sides.[37]

French protection of the native population could have been improved in two possible ways. One was the totalitarian solution of thorough social regimentation, based on the possession of superior force, which Trinquier and some other *guerre-révolutionnaire* theorists favored. However, metropolitan France would never have consented to making Algeria a vast concentration camp, for both ethical and economic reasons. On the other hand, SAS-SAU programs could have been transformed and expanded into a sincere attempt to organize and aid the Muslim population. Yet, as a student of the subject observed, political conditions in Algeria were properly the concern of the civilian government, not of the military: "Basic reform was a domain in which the government, not the army, should have been expected to provide leadership."[38] Effective protection of the population from indigenous terrorism required an intimate contact that politicized the military when the task was relegated to it. Any relationship the army established with the population that provided the basis for efficient protection, whether of domination by force or of mutual confidence, caused political change. The Algerian case illustrates the danger to a democratic regime of thrusting this responsibility onto the military. Terrorism is a political problem that must be solved on a political rather than a military basis, and to check terrorism the government must be willing to consider its causes as well as the conditions that make it possible.

The French offensive response to FLN terrorism was an energetic attempt to seek out and destroy the FLN's parallel administration (the OPA), the ALN guerrilla bands, and the urban terrorist commandos. This strategy suited the army better than the defensive strategy of protecting populations, but even an offensive strategy resembled police work, and the army preferred open and conventional combat.

The key to an effective attack on any underground organization is intelligence, and this the French military and police lacked. Their ignorance strengthened a tendency to regard all Algerians as suspects, since the guilty could not be distinguished from the innocent. One reason for the lack of information was the unprotected Algerian population's fear of FLN retaliation, and this cause-and-effect relationship linked offensive to defensive strategy in a vicious circle. In the absence of spontaneous information, the French army resorted to brutal interrogation methods to extract information about the FLN. The recommended practice was to obtain information from suspects as rapidly as possible, through the use of torture if necessary, and to exploit such intelligence immediately, regardless of any standards of legality. The army assumed that all suspects (therefore all Algerians) knew something about the FLN organization, if only the identity of the funds collector in their area. All successive commanders-in-chief in Algeria, as well as Governors-General Soustelle and Lacoste, approved the use of torture.

Opinions on the efficiency of torture as a means of intelligence gathering were sharply divided. Most of the *guerre-révolutionnaire* theorists considered torture the only valid response to insurgent terrorism. Colonel Trinquier argued that "the use of terrorism as a weapon of war inevitably provokes the utilization of its antidote, torture. It is a reality which the rebellion should take into account."[39] He insisted that it is rarely necessary to use torture, however, since the threat of it is often enough to make suspects talk.[40] Either the value of torture as a threat was low, or most interrogators were incapable of subtlety, since the army commonly practiced physical torture of suspects. Another proponent of torture, the chaplain to General Massu's paratrooper regiments, regarded its use as necessary to "disarm" the terrorist of his knowledge because he intends to "kill unjustly."[41]

Other military authorities were less certain of the utility of torture, but they accepted it nonetheless. One French officer admitted that it was morally wrong to threaten a person's life or to humiliate him with torture, but said that if a suspect under questioning knew where a bomb that was about to go off was located, the interrogator who did not discover that information was an accomplice of the assassin. On the other hand, the argument continued, when no such state of emergency existed, when the army was questioning, for example, a peasant whom the FLN visited at night, it would be hypocritical or foolish not to torture, because the army was required to find out anything anyone knew about the adversary.[42] The argument that torture was an essential response to life-or-death issues was patently false, since cases of drastic urgency were rare in the Algerian conflict, but many practitioners of torture obviously felt a need to excuse their conduct in this dramatic fashion.

There are numerous drawbacks to the use of torture. Aside from the ethical and humane implications, voluntary information is much more reliable. Torture is also psychologically harmful for both torturers and victims. A journalist described the methods used by the French in Algiers: "It is certain that without torture the F.L.N.'s terrorist network would never have been overcome; it is equally certain that the degrading effect on those who used it and its hideous consequences on the thousands of innocent Algerians subjected to it outweighed in importance the 'battle of Algiers' itself."[43] The use of torture in Algeria also shocked major parts of French and international opinion and drew sympathetic attention to the FLN's cause. Many liberals wisely reminded the government at the time that by failing to punish atrocities and cruelty, they forfeited the right to condemn such acts.[44]

Ten years after the end of the war in Algeria, the publication of General Massu's memoirs revived the still-heated debate in France over the use of torture in Algeria.[45] The reopening of this controversy demonstrates the powerful political effects a colonial war can have on the metropolis. Massu frankly admitted the institutionalized and systematic use of torture, an admission that no official had dared to make at the time. He justified torture by condemning terrorism and added: "There were few errors affecting the innocent; in very few cases did we arrest, interrogate, and beat up individuals who had nothing to do with terrorism."[46] In his complacency, which was based on the conclusions that torture was mild compared to FLN savagery, and all of the suspects were guilty, Massu noted only two possible ill effects of torture (which he did not consider in the least dangerous for the victim despite certain unavoidable "accidents"). First, Massu believed that torture was morally dangerous for the torturer, and that the period of service in this field should be limited. His account failed to explain why torture is risky for the torturer if it is not morally degrading or physically harmful for the victim. Second, Massu recognized the danger of uncontrolled civilian imitation of military practices and feared an "unhealthy psychosis" among the European population.[47] His concern did not extend to the mental or physical health of the principal victims of torture.

Massu's outspoken defense of torture could not fail to arouse rebuttals, and four critical replies soon appeared. Jules Roy, a well-known novelist and liberal of Algerian origin and the author of an earlier study of the Algerian war, was the first to lash out in an emotional and personal polemic against Massu.[48] Pierre Vidal-Naquet, the leader of the original antitorture campaign in France in 1957, published a study of torture in England and Italy that was revised for publication in France only in 1972.[49] This well-documented work contended that torture was an institution among both the police and the army in Algeria and that the highest political authorities condoned it while refusing to accept the responsibility for its consequences. Vidal-Naquet concluded that the 1958 change of regime modified neither the use of torture nor the "cover" given it by governmental authorities. Nor was torture restricted to Algeria; the metropolitan police practiced it extensively against Algerians in France.[50] The French judicial establishment was guilty at least of complicity with the police and military, and few torturers were ever brought to trial, or if they were, condemned.

The third response to General Massu, General Jacques Pâris de Bollardière's memoirs, is particularly interesting since General Bollardière confronted the same situation in Algeria as Massu, but chose a different response.[51] The only French officer publicly to refuse to use torture, he vehemently condemned Massu's arguments about the efficiency and justification of brutality: "Torture degrades the one who inflicts it even more than the one who suffers it. The reasons for ceding to the practice of violence and torture can only be explained by the impotence of the torturers."[52] Bollardière felt that establishing a climate of security and confidence between French and Algerians would be more profitable than coercion, although he realized that it was probably too late by then for a real dialogue between the two communities in Algeria.[53] General Bollardière's anti-FLN program, which included providing work for the unemployed population and waging counterguerrilla operations, could report only seven French soldiers killed and a noticeable decrease in terrorism after five months of action. However, Bollardière's successes were constantly jeopardized by the troops of neighboring sectors, who did not hesitate to arrest or execute residents of his area. The incomprehension, if not active hostility, of his superior officers was clearly revealed when Bollardière learned that Defense Minister Max Lejeune formally disapproved of his methods, that no more funds were to be made available for the public-works program, and that there would be no replacements for his troops when they finished their periods of service. Immediately thereafter, Bollardière received direct orders from Massu, who was in control of the entire Algiers region, that "police operations" were to take precedence over "pacification." Bollardière protested personally to Massu, to Commander-in-Chief Salan, and to Governor-General Lacoste, and then asked to be relieved of his command.[54] When he publicly criticized Algerian policy, he was sentenced to two months of fortress arrest.

Bollardière's account of the war correctly pointed out that although Massu's mission was to maintain security and to reconcile the two communities of Algeria, Massu did not realize that the restoration of order did not automatically create Algerian confidence. Massu thought only of the European population and underestimated Algerian nationalism. According to Bollardière, Massu should have established direct contacts with the FLN leaders in an attempt to halt terrorism as Germaine Tillion had done with positive results in the summer of 1957.[55]

The fourth response to Massu's reflections on the Battle of Algiers came from the onetime head of the FFFLN, Mohamed Lebjaoui, who accused Massu of attempting to justify practices that were war crimes if not acts of genocide.[56] Lebjaoui pointed out that although Massu pretended that torture was only used against the insurgents, it was actually used against all Algerians, innocent and guilty alike, to expose the FLN organization. Furthermore, Massu obscured the fact that torture was fundamentally a method of dehumanization, that it was used not only to "make someone talk" but also to humiliate an entire community of people and to convince them of their inferiority. Torture was thus the very essence of colonialism.[57]

Lebjaoui also refused to accept Massu's excuse that torture was a response to FLN terrorism:

> To pretend that the campaign of blind terror known as the "Battle of Algiers" was only a reply to a "terrorism" itself blind initiated by the F.L.N. is ignominious because it is a historical countertruth. The dates and facts are there: no bomb struck the civilian population of Algiers before Algerian blood was shed. And if errors were committed on our side, they can be explained by the conditions of our struggle. But the F.L.N. led, fundamentally, a political combat. To this was opposed only the arms of repression.[58]

As Lebjaoui contended, torture was not only a means of obtaining intelligence, but also a way of terrorizing Algerians and making the cost of aiding the FLN greater than the risks of refusing to do so. A substantial part of the army probably believed, as the *guerre-révolutionnaire* advocates did, that the Algerian population only obeyed the FLN because they feared it more than the French. The certainty of torture for those who collaborated with the FLN if they were arrested by the French was seen as a deterrent to rebellion and a counterbalance to FLN threats. Torture could also be a means of irrational vengeance for FLN atrocities. The government and the higher military authorities permitted the practice by putting effective control of interrogations into the hands of lower-level officers and enlisted men who were directly involved in combat operations, and covering and excusing all torture as an unfortunate necessity of intelligence gathering during an internal war.

During the early part of the war, the army often became disgusted with the tedious processes of civilian justice. Since the government had not declared a state of war in Algeria (in accordance with one of the basic asymmetries of revolutionary war), all suspects were legally entitled to appear before the regular courts. The result—not an unusual one in Algeria—was a situation of tacitly accepted illegality, with the military taking justice into its own hands. Summary execution of suspects became common, before or after their arrest and interrogation. By the demise of the Fourth Republic, almost all of Algeria was under martial law.

De Gaulle tried to correct the abuses of military justice, as well as to halt the use of torture, by reforming the civilian judicial system after the 1960 revolt in Algiers (the Barricades Affair). However, six years of war had done untold damage to the French reputation and de Gaulle lacked sufficient authority over the military. Besides arbitrary executions, many other forms of illegal violence were used that terrorized and alienated the Algerian population, such as bombings of villages suspected of sympathy for the FLN and random raids into Algerian quarters, often in retaliation for FLN terrorism. The French may have regarded these as acts of vengeance, but from the FLN point of view, they were irrational and indiscriminate reprisals provoked by terrorism.

Although both offensive and defensive military strategies are generally meant to prevent the initial commission of acts of terrorism, the government can thwart the intended psychological effect of these acts once they are committed by limiting publicity about them. A democratic government must weigh the benefits to be gained from censorship against the dangers, such as its increased vulnerability to accusations of infringement of freedom of expression. It must also reconcile its desire to emphasize the opponents' atrocities, which testify to their unfitness as the country's future leaders, with the aim of denying them the publicity they seek. A moderate approach—one that allows the publication of information about terrorism but discourages sensational exploitation of the issue—is probably the best choice. In this age of instantaneous communications, extreme measures are not only difficult to implement, but probably self-defeating in the end. In France the policy of seizing journals and charging journalists with crimes aroused acrimonious public debate; it probably sensitized elements of opinion that had heretofore remained apathetic. Commenting on French policy, one author declared that "it seems unlikely that a policy which was so haphazardly conceived and erratically executed could have borne much fruit"; instead it alerted the public to what the government wanted to conceal.[59]

In the French case, limiting publicity about terrorism was less important than preventing the terrorists from provoking the military and the European civilians to irrational violence. Tolerance of such reprisals showed the government's inability or unwillingness to give Algerians the same protection from terrorism as Europeans. The damage that "spontaneous" outbreaks against the Algerians did to the French cause is incalculable. The police and the military were not disciplined enough to prevent outrages by their own ranks, much less by civilians with whom they often sympathized. The government further diminished its credibility by maintaining that such incidents were isolated and rare and that those responsible for them were always punished. On this issue there was little difference between the Fourth and Fifth Republics. De Gaulle certainly disapproved of indiscriminate violence and torture, but since he was forced to concentrate on regaining political power from the military and civilian extremist groups, he was unable to control or use the police and military as instruments against civilian anti-Algerian aggression. The fact that the Paris government had to import metropolitan special police (*les barbouzes*) to Algeria to crush the OAS illustrates the fragility of de Gaulle's hold.

CONCLUSIONS

French policy in Algeria was limited by factors that are common to most regimes faced with a revolutionary war. The government lost the initiative and was forced onto the defensive; its authority was seriously challenged. Under stress, the government's choice of alternative policies was further limited by weaknesses in the decision-making process, particularly the government's sensitivity to reactionary interest groups and its inability to formulate clear goals for its Algerian policy in the critical period 1954–1958.

Thus the antiterrorist policies that were actually implemented in Algeria were oriented toward military means and toward the needs of the European minority rather than those of the Algerian majority. The military view of the war in Algeria was strongly influenced by *guerre-révolutionnaire* theories, which superficially characterized the insurrection as a Communist-sponsored manipulation of a passive and apathetic population. Military policy in Algeria, concentrating on offensive strategy and the security of Europeans, failed to protect Algerians from FLN violence or to shield them from the revolutionaries' organizational and propaganda activities. The government's ostensible efforts to guard the Algerians, such as the resettlement of populations, only aggravated the situation. The brutal, indiscriminate, and illegal repression of opposition alienated the Algerian people and drove them into the arms of the FLN. French violence also had self-defeating political consequences in metropolitan France and abroad. Punishment, often in the form of physical torture, was meted out to guilty and innocent alike, in contrast to the more discriminating and subtle violence of the FLN.

The Fourth Republic could neither implement nor promise political reforms that would have effectively removed the FLN's justification for terrorism as its only way of expressing its grievances. That the government reacted to the prospect of an FLN-sponsored strike in 1957 by calling in the army to break the strike was indicative of a general policy that, by denying the opposition legitimate means of expression, encouraged the FLN to resort to violence. By the time de Gaulle was strong enough to offer free elections and universal suffrage, it was too late for reforms to be meaningful.

In 1958 a French observer lamented the dilemma confronting democracies: the only defense against terrorism appeared to be the adoption of methods such as torture and repression that negated the ideals a democratic government stands for.[60] Yet this problem was false in the case of the Algerian revolution, since after 1957, democracy in Algeria would have given the country to the FLN just as effectively as the 1962 Evian Accords did. France was a democracy, but the majority of Algerians were excluded from its benefits despite the legal fiction of "integration." The FLN succeeded and the French failed precisely because the Algerian system was one of colonial authoritarianism, but the French government was susceptible to the pressures of public opinion. There was no possibility of European acceptance of a democratic solution in Algeria, as the support for the OAS in 1961–1962 illustrated. Nor were the military and police reliable vehicles for de Gaulle's attempts to generate a moderate Algerian "third force," an idea that was probably outdated by the time it was proposed. It is extremely difficult for a terrorist movement to gain the degree of popular support that is necessary to sustain its activities unless the government fails to satisfy genuine popular grievances or is powerless to protect the population from terrorism, but the French government managed to combine unresponsiveness with impotence. Although the FLN was militarily defeated by the French army, the cost of containing and developing a restless territory under the constant threat of terrorism was too high a price for the metropolitan public to pay. The conscripts who fought the war were drafted from France, the financial cost of the war was paid by the metropole, and the political responsibility for fighting an increasingly unpopular war lay with the French government. Once de Gaulle regained control after the 1961 putsch, he sacrificed Algeria so that he could pursue foreign-policy goals that were incompatible with a colonial war.

The Strategy of Terrorism: Conclusions

VIII

Revolutionary terrorism is a drive for political power. The resort to terrorism is a political choice, not an act of madness. Terrorism is a specific strategy, a distinctive pattern of violence that can be understood and analyzed in terms of logical objectives and observable consequences. What causes a revolutionary movement to select a method based on creating fear and horror? Is terrorism an effective revolutionary strategy? To what extent can a case study of the FLN answer these questions?

The context of terrorism is an important factor in explaining its use, and the Algerian case presents certain unique features; even though each case of terrorism occurs within a discrete set of historical events, comparison and classification of objective background conditions should be possible. While historical circumstances may contribute to the use of terrorism, however, they are not its immediate causes. The FLN's motivation for its reliance on terrorism deserves close consideration. The general pattern of terrorism—an overview of how FLN terrorism worked—is also important to understanding the strategy. Finally, an evaluation of the success or failure of terrorism must consider the political ends it accomplished and the relationship between terrorism and the FLN's ultimate victory in the struggle for Algerian independence.

THE ALGERIAN CONTEXT

The concept of colonialism sums up the scene against which FLN terrorism was outlined. In Algeria, the colonial system, with its convenient and visible class distinctions, the powerlessness and poverty of the colonized majority, and the willful determination of the colonizers to cling to the privileges of the dominant class, provided the FLN with an emotional reservoir of mutual suspicion and a ready-made cleavage— social, cultural, religious, racial, economic, and above all political—to exploit. The stress of violence could only widen the gulf between the two communities. The identity of the "enemy" did not have to be established for an Algerian population whose grievances were painfully real.

The cause of national independence was naturally attractive to the Algerian victims of alien injustice, who saw their attempts at participation in politics and society rejected out of hand by the French government under pressure by the colon lobbyists. By 1954, many Algerian nationalists had decided that political progress was impossible under French rule, but the ideology of nationalism had not yet stimulated the traditional, politically apathetic, and poverty-stricken Algerian population to action. Mass revolution was a future possibility, not a present reality. All the necessary prerevolutionary conditions existed; what was needed was a catalyst, and the efforts of the FLN provided it. Terrorism became one means of mobilizing the Algerian people and forcing them to participate in political decisions by choosing one side or the other in the war for independence.

The circumstances of colonialism also dictated the terms of the paradox that was the French response—a policy that brought disaster because of its own contradictions. On the one hand, the government in Paris and its administration in Algiers were blind to the vulnerability, both physical and emotional, of their Algerian subjects. The predominant influence of the colons on French policy and the corresponding failure of the civil administration to penetrate the countryside had isolated the government from the non-European population well before 1954. A mixture of neglect and arrogance characterized European attitudes. Yet on the other hand, the government in Paris was enormously sensitive to the demands of its constituency. Although at first this meant allowing the interests of the settlers to dominate Algerian policy and tolerating military disobedience that culminated in revolt, it ultimately meant that opposition in France to the war required a settlement. The political system of Algeria itself was authoritarian and, when it was advantageous to the regime, illegal by its own standards, but democracy in France, the colonial metropolis, was the key to the eventual resolution of the struggle. Tension between the demands of the entrenched colonial elite in Algeria, often supported by the French military, and the French people kept the congenitally weak Fourth Republic on the verge of breakdown. When the government did succumb to this combination of forces, the same constraints hampered de Gaulle's settlement of the problem. Because the regime was responsive to pressure, and because the state's resources were finite, the war could be made too costly. Terrorism was a significant factor in raising the price to the French of combatting Algerian nationalism.

The conditions of international political life in the 1950s must also be considered in an explanation of FLN terrorism. Nationalism and anticolonialism aroused sympathetic responses in diplomatic circles, particularly in view of the dramatic changes that were occurring in the composition of the United Nations. France was withdrawing from Indochina, Tunisia, and Morocco. Egypt threw the British out in 1956, and Nasser promoted revolution throughout the Arab world. The FLN could profit from a growing anticolonial sentiment and from the support of an increasing number of newly independent states, while France was inevitably placed on the defensive. France was isolated on the diplomatic front, abandoned even by her Western allies, particularly the United States.

In sum, then, Algerian terrorism was set against a colonial background. The society in question was divided between a relatively large, indigenous European settler elite and a vast native majority who had legitimate grievances against the government but no possibility of peaceful redress. The Algerian setting was revolutionary—a propitious environment for the development of a mass-based nationalistic movement. It was also a situation in which the resistance movement could solicit tangible external assistance. By making Algerian policy an issue in metropolitan politics, the war raised a critical question: in whose interests were decisions about Algeria to be made? With a competition for influence thus opened, it became inevitable that the citizens of the French metropole would overrule the colon pressure groups who had determined the French government's actions in Algeria for so long.

These background factors are useful in a comparative sense. In the two decades following the Second World War, there were many instances of terrorism in a colonial setting, although none that was quite identical to the situation in Algeria: the Palestine Mandate, Indochina, Morocco, Tunisia, Cyprus, Malaya, South Arabia, and Kenya. A similar situation today is that of the Provisional IRA in Northern Ireland, since the government to be influenced is in London, not Ulster. Yet in most cases in the 1960s and 1970s, terrorists have had to reckon directly with an independent government. In Israel and in Rhodesia, the settlers themselves now hold the reins of power; their survival is at stake, as it was not for the colonial government in a distant metropolis. Another distinction involves the kind of society in which terrorism occurs— whether it is divided or homogeneous. Northern Ireland and Rhodesia are examples of polarized states; in more homogeneous societies, dissidents may use terrorism to try to revive old divisions or invent new ones. Regional separatist movements, such as that of the Basques, are relevant here. Yet another point of comparison is the degree to which opposition is tolerated in the affected polity. Terrorism in a democratic system that permits open dissent and terrorism in an authoritarian regime that does not may be two different phenomena. A related point is whether the terrorists represent serious popular grievances. (Of course, even in a system in which grievances may be freely expressed, the government may not be able to satisfy them.) In a sense, this is a distinction between a potential for full-scale revolution and a potential for limited rebellion or revolt.

THE CAUSES OF TERRORISM

Why do revolutionary movements choose to use terrorism? An answer to this question must distinguish between the causes of revolution in general and the causes of terrorism in particular. Not all internal wars have included terrorism; the Cuban and Chinese revolutions were successful, mass-based, violent revolutions without the terror that characterized the Algerian revolution. The motives for the initial resort to terrorism, in its different forms, differ from the incentives for continuing a strategy of terrorism once it gains its own momentum. Revolutionary leaders do not plan ahead in detail for years of struggle; many later decisions are ad hoc and reactive. However, the initial decision to open the conflict with terrorism is decisive.

Terrorists are basically rational, in the sense that they perform acts of terrorism as means to political ends. In the case of the FLN, the dominant reason for choosing terrorism appears to have been its expected utility in achieving the insurgents' goals, despite the unquestionable influences of psychological, social, and organizational factors.

For example, the premium the FLN placed on both the reality and the appearance of internal unity was significant, although, especially during the period of negotiations that terminated the war, factions within the resistance movement used terrorism for their private political ends. Rivalry between the FLN's political and military bureaucracies and the decentralized structure of the revolutionary organization, which permitted the exercise of independent authority by the wilaya commanders, were the most important organizational factors. In social-psychological terms, violence was usually not an end in itself for FLN members. Although passions and prejudices—for example, xenophobia, alienation, anger, revenge, and conceptions of honor—influenced the FLN's decisions, the links between individual personalities and the decisions to use terrorism were weak.[1] This gap between an emotional inclination to use violence and a decision to perform an act of terrorism was caused in part by the operational lag between decision making at the higher echelons of the FLN organization and the actual implementation of these decisions by lower-level cadres. The FLN's relatively tight control over its organizational networks, which was perhaps stronger at the regional than at the national level, contributed to the discipline that made terrorism more of a rational than an irrational activity. In addition, both high-level FLN decision makers and the terrorists who executed their directions came from diverse backgrounds—students from a privileged milieu, members of the urban working class, the unemployed, peasants, even criminals—and therefore there was no unique "terrorist personality" or specific class background. This is not to say that certain psychological types were not attracted to the danger and the excitement of the life of the terrorist, but that their personal motivations were not the reasons for the FLN's choice of a strategy of terrorism. Social, psychological, and organizational considerations were intervening rather than independent variables. They undoubtedly affected the actual forms terrorism took in Algeria (for example, throat cutting and mutilation of the face) but they were not the central determinants of the choice of terrorism over other alternatives.

The key motivation for terrorism in a context in which the normal means of access to government (elections, political parties, interest groups, strikes or demonstrations) were denied was a willingness by the FLN to accept high risks and a considerable inequality of power between the revolutionary movement and the French regime. The absolute determination of the revolutionary elite was based on the intrinsic merit of the goal of independence as well as the fact that its expected benefits were obtainable only through violence. In addition, the FLN's aspirations were realistic; success seemed relatively likely, given the corresponding events in other colonies, both French and British. Struggles for freedom elsewhere, particularly in neighboring Tunisia and Morocco, served as inspiration to the FLN and also as challenge. What could one say of the honor of the Algerians if they stagnated passively under French rule while their brother Arabs and other oppressed peoples threw off the colonial yoke?

Terrorism, a low-cost and easily implemented strategy, was the only feasible alternative for the new nationalist organization because the FLN lacked *both* the necessary material resources (money, arms, soldiers) *and* active popular support. When a committed core of leaders agreed that violence was the only solution to the impasse in which they found themselves, their inability to push the mass of the Algerian people into open opposition or to mount large-scale guerrilla warfare encouraged them to adopt a strategy of terrorism. It is in this sense that terrorism is the weapon of the weak, the result of desperation and despair. Terrorism was an attempt to acquire political power through unusual means. Its users accepted risk and danger because of the importance of their goal and the absence of choice.

A further incentive to FLN terrorism was the French violence of the past. References to the wrongs done to Algerians by the colonial regime served as emotional justification for violence against the enemy, especially civilians. Evoking an image of Algerian suffering under colon domination undoubtedly assuaged feelings of guilt and released inhibitions. These accusations were also part of a propaganda campaign to excuse the resort to terrorism. Blaming the French for the neglect, cruelty, and illegitimacy of years of colonial rule and appealing for independence from this oppression took on a dual role as both motivation and rationalization.

What general application do these observations about the causes of FLN terrorism have? The revolutionaries of the FLN turned to terrorism in the opening stages of the war because they were determined to act, they saw no other way of getting what they wanted, and they thought terrorism would work. The choice of terrorism was a result of their perception of the situation; in their particular case this judgement turned out to be astute, but terrorism may not be the best choice in other situations. Although terrorists may genuinely believe that they have no alternative, a dispassionate observer may be able to find other paths to the same end. Insurgents may think that terrorism will work to influence their audiences when it will not. In any case, both the people who decide to use terrorism and the people who follow their orders are extreme risk takers, whatever their reasons for choosing this course.

THE PROCESSES OF TERRORISM

The character of the FLN and the nature of its struggle imposed two distinctive features on the process of terrorism in Algeria. First, the FLN did not rely almost entirely on terrorism as other limited resistance movements have done—the Zionist Irgun, the Cypriot EOKA, the Baader-Meinhof group, and the Tupamaros, among many others. Terrorism was employed in conjunction with other forms of violence, especially rural guerrilla warfare, and with nonviolent tactics, including propaganda, diplomacy, and the establishment of a mass political organization, a countergovernment that was more effective than the French administration. The FLN was an ideologically broad and politically synthetic movement, incorporating any nationalists who accepted its leadership. Its recruits, both leaders and cadres, were the most skilled, talented, articulate, and experienced human resources that Algeria had to offer. The FLN successfully linked a French-educated elite typified by Ferhat Abbas, who became president of the provisional government although he was late in joining the struggle, with rough soldier-bandits like the Kabyle Belkacem Krim. Coordinated with a full panoply of political and military stratagems, terrorism was integral to the revolution. It served major political objectives: the acquisition of popular support, the destruction of the colonial regime in Algeria, the maintenance of morale and discipline within the FLN, and the projection of an image of strength and determination abroad.

The most significant attribute of FLN terrorism—one that was not common to other revolutionary methods, was its political multifunctionality. A single action, such as a bombing in Algiers, simultaneously served several political purposes. Almost every individual act of terrorism must be interpreted from different perspectives and gains new meaning with each angle of approach. This multifaceted character also increases the attractiveness of terrorism as a means of gaining political influence.

This multifunctionality resulted from the fact that an act of terrorism had concurrent effects on several separate audiences, both direct (those who identify with the victim of violence) and indirect (spectators who are not physically threatened). In terms of each specific political objective, one audience, whether direct or indirect, was of primary importance. For example, an analysis of the effects of a bombing in Algiers in terms of Algerian support for the FLN might overlook secondary reactions from audiences abroad. But from the perspective of terrorism as a means of creating an image, its political impact on domestic populations was significant only as it visibly enhanced the FLN's appearance of representativeness and strength. This observation holds true for other cases of terrorism. For example, the Black September attack on Israeli athletes at Munich in 1972 could be interpreted as a gesture of intimidation toward Israelis, but this would be an inadequate analysis.

Responses to terrorism sometimes have a multiplying effect. The original act of terrorism provokes an active response from one audience, and this response in turn stimulates a reaction in a second audience. Distinguishing between the reaction to the initial act of terrorism and the reaction to the effects of terrorism is complicated. For example, provocation terrorism required violence from the direct audience—the European or French enemy—against Algerians to inspire their sympathy for the FLN and their hatred for the French; thus the assumption that European riots were the sole consequence of FLN terrorism would be misleading. Likewise, Israeli reprisals against Palestinian refugee camps have had a much greater political impact than the destruction they caused, and the West German government's antisubversive measures may be more serious in the long run than the terrorism that provoked their adoption.

The continuation of the strategy of terrorism over a period of time encouraged a learning process. Their experience with terrorism taught the FLN leaders definite lessons about its usefulness. When a particular type of terrorism proved to be effective, it might be continued regardless of the original motivation. Even terrorism that was accidental or the result of a breakdown in communications between regions and the center, such as the August 1955 *jacquerie* in the Constantinois district, was repeated if the unintended consequences turned out to be functional. Observation and subsequent imitation of successes meant that the process of terrorism acquired a momentum independent of the causes that initiated the original choice. For instance, it could be argued that after 1958 the FLN was no longer motivated by weakness. The de Gaulle government held open elections in which all nationalists were invited to participate, and the FLN possessed substantial popular support and financial resources. Yet terrorism continued, partly because it had worked in the past and partly because the social and moral restraints against its use had crumbled. After their initial experience with terrorism, the FLN leaders and cadres possessed a cognitive framework for rationalizing and explaining its causes and its consequences. Thus its continuation was both rational (because knowledge of the cost-benefit ratio had become more certain) and irrational (because subconscious taboos had been eroded, and the performance of acts of terrorism by then required fewer and less explicit justifications, such as "we had no other choice").

The converse implication of this process of "learning through doing" is that the failure of a particular type of terrorism should cause revolutionary decision makers to abandon or modify its use. Since terrorism is multifunctional, however, failure to promote one objective might be outweighed by successes in other areas. In any case, the FLN's campaign to "bring the war home" to France in 1958 was never repeated because it aroused antagonism toward the FLN instead of popular opposition to the war. Hostility toward Algerians in France could serve no useful purpose, since the FLN's major enemy there was not the French but the MNA. The FLN also needed the assistance of French liberals such as those in the "Jeanson Network," who transported FLN funds from France to Switzerland.

Learning through experience can also explain the phenomenon of imitation, which has been so prevalent in modern transnational terrorist strategy. Aircraft hijackings, diplomatic kidnappings, the seizure of schoolchildren as hostages—all are copied by dissident groups of varying ideological persuasions and spread from continent to continent. The publicity surrounding terrorism impresses other groups with both the possibility and the utility of terrorism. Especially if a resistance movement perceives its situation and goals as similar to those of the original revolutionaries, success (which may be more a matter of image than of reality) tempts it to imitation. Terrorism is thereby removed further from motivations of deprivation and desperation, although these justifications for terrorist acts have acquired liturgical status in resistance pronouncements. Terrorism is not always a spontaneous and daring response to circumstances of inequality and scarce alternatives; it can be purely contrived, artificial, and calculating. The motive of utility can become dominant. Radical groups on the right or the left turn to terrorism before exhausting other possibilities because it is available and has apparently worked for others. The imitation factor helps to explain the phenomenon of terrorism against democratic governments, as practiced by the Baader-Meinhof group in West Germany or by the South Moluccan independence movement in the Netherlands. Opponents of terrorism would do well to publicize its failures as much as its successes, if they can distinguish one from the other.

The FLN's strategy of terrorism depended upon the influence acts of violence had on recognizable audiences whose emotional and political responses were significant in terms of the FLN's goals. The actual form the violence took depended on the identity and size of the audience and on the desired reaction. The spectrum of psychological responses to terrorism can be distinguished in terms of whether audiences were direct or indirect. Direct audiences who were threatened by terrorism were likely to experience terror, fear, hostility, respect, or a combination of these emotions. Reactions ranging from respect through curiosity, admiration, and satisfaction were appropriate to indirect audiences, who were spectators rather than prospective victims. People who are likely to be attacked themselves naturally experience stronger emotions. However, the distinction between audiences whose invulnerability is only transitory—that is, who may be victims for other types of terrorism at another time—and indirect audiences who are physically secure because of distance from the struggle may be significant. Can the unthreatened audience regard terrorism as a drama that is immediately affecting but in the long run unreal and abstract? Does curiosity predominate, regardless of shock or of political predispositions toward one side or the other? Or do all audiences for terrorism feel a personal and intimate threat?

The FLN's use of terrorism demonstrated that the responses of the indirect audiences were as important to the revolutionary cause as the reactions of the direct audiences. The need to reach indirect audiences may be a reason for the adoption of increasingly spectacular violence by modern terrorist groups. Present-day terrorists rely more extensively on the tactics of pressure and maneuver, on influencing third parties to compel their opponent to concede, than the FLN did. Terrorists with such an imperative demand the attention of the world audience, of people who are unsympathetic to, or unaware of, their cause. Terrorism to attract and inform diverse and distant audiences, who may today be jaded with violence, escalates to higher levels of destructiveness and outrageousness.

FLN leaders consistently tried to avoid acts of terrorism that might anger audiences whose support they needed and could realistically expect, such as the metropolitan population and even the European population of Algeria before 1956. Terrorism was directed against the Algerian population as a heterogeneous rather than a homogeneous target—that is, violence was aimed at specific subgroups within the population: rival elites, the disobedient, or overt supporters of the French. Only in 1956 when the European audience showed itself to be unanimously and adamantly opposed to any compromise did the FLN leaders, who had also learned from August 1955 that mass-casualty terrorism against Europeans earned international attention, focus on Europeans as a stereotyped enemy. The prominence of the European population as a target was increased by the sharp delineation of social and ethnic boundaries within Algerian society. The visibility and the size of the group, which made it possible to isolate the Europeans from the general population, also enhanced their value as victims, and their close association with the French regime, inevitable and sometimes unwanted though it was, conveniently linked civilians and government as a common enemy.

Terrorism against Europeans frequently took the form of spectacular, high-casualty violence because all Europeans were lumped together as the "enemy" and thus all became eligible victims. Europeans became an undifferentiated, homogeneous direct audience; attacks on any member of this class were acceptable. Such violence was "indiscriminate" only within these limits. The FLN could bomb a restaurant frequented by Europeans with assurance that the meaning of the act would be clear because the identity of the victims was unambiguous. A truly "indiscriminate" act that affected victims from a mixture of audiences would not have had this clarity. High-casualty terrorism was extremely multifunctional for the FLN because of its publicity value. Violence against limited subgroups of the Algerian audience was of less value, partly because "native" victims were much less newsworthy, but also because the FLN did not want to alienate potential supporters.

The FLN usually issued warnings or statements about terrorism that stereotyped its victims as "traitors" or "enemies," blamed the French for initiating violence, stressed the avenging nature of terrorism, and portrayed individual terrorists as self-sacrificing heroes. These ideological communications can be interpreted as attempts to justify violence to audiences whose acceptance the FLN needed. The FLN's release of kidnapping victims can also be viewed as a means of making violence less objectionable—creating acute anxiety followed by dramatic relief. The FLN did not employ the tactic of kidnapping for political ransom, although it did execute French military captives in retaliation for the French execution of FLN prisoners.

The FLN's discrimination in choosing its audiences and concern for legitimizing the selection of victims were of enormous importance. Such refinement is apparently alien to the calculations of many modern terrorist groups. Over the past century, terrorists have broadened the range of influential audiences and thus of eligible victims. Through the progression from assassinating government officials to eliminating traitors, then to attacking enemy civilians, and finally to deliberately targeting victims who are the least powerful (or the most innocent of responsibility), murderers are becoming less delicate.[2]

Throughout the war, the FLN employed terrorism to undermine the authority of rival elites, including the French government, although indigenous leaders of similar nationalist persuasion were considered the most dangerous adversaries. Intolerance for political rivals was linked to the FLN's insistence on being the *seul interlocuteur valable* or representative of the Algerian people, as well as to its desire to maintain a unified resistance movement. The nationalists who made the revolution were determined to avoid the futile internal quarrels that had sapped the strength of their predecessors.

Some incidents of modern terrorism may also be attributable to a struggle for power within the resistance movement. For example, between April and June 1974, the Palestinian resistance was responsible for four major attacks within Israel. The first was an attack by the Popular Front for the Liberation of Palestine–General Command (PFLP–GC), a small extremist faction, on the settlement of Qiryat Shemona. Sixteen Israeli civilians were killed, including eight children. The main purpose of this publicity-seeking violence was to undercut any compromise the Palestine Liberation Organization (PLO), to which the PFLP–GC belonged, might make. Shortly thereafter the Popular Democratic Front for the Liberation of Palestine, an equally extreme group on the left, struck at a school in Maalot. Its objective was to assert its power within the resistance and to block any impending Arab-Israeli settlement. Not to be outdone, the PFLP–GC soon responded with an attack on an Israeli kibbutz. Finally, to avoid losing control of the resistance and being associated with "defeatism," the hitherto abstentionist Fatah, which is the dominant element in the PLO and had recently been critical of extremist terrorism, struck at the Israeli town of Nahariya.[3] This wave of terrorism was partly a response to the impending Egyptian-Israeli disengagement accords, but the series of raids, particularly the attack by Fatah, is incomprehensible unless the internal politics of the Palestinian resistance are taken into account.

The FLN placed a premium on maintaining the unity and coherence of the revolutionary organization because centrifugal forces were dangerously strong. Therefore the central leadership followed a policy of accepting responsibility for unauthorized acts of terrorism that were committed on the initiative of local or regional leaders. Only if the consequences of terrorism were extremely harmful to the cause, especially if negative publicity abroad resulted, did the FLN leaders deny their subordinates' actions, as in the case of Melouza, and such denials were rare. The high degree of decentralization and local independence in the FLN organization allowed much locally directed terrorism, but it is a tribute to the FLN's organizational efforts that despite the fragmentation caused by the geographical size of Algeria and the constant French military pressure, there was little of the disunity and disruptive autonomous terrorism that has characterized the Palestinian resistance. Fatah has also followed a different verbal strategy. While denouncing acts of terrorism performed by the extremists, Fatah leaders have tried to excuse and justify these acts by referring to the plight of the Palestinians, which drove them to violence in desperation.[4] The South Moluccan terrorism in the Netherlands in 1976–1977 also prompted the respectable elder leaders of the South Moluccan community to decry the abhorrent methods of the terrorists, but at the same time their cause profited by the world attention attracted by the terrorists.

The FLN's decision to use spectacular terrorism against European civilians was the subject of great controversy within the leadership. The need for international recognition dominated the decision making that led to the Battle of Algiers, but the choice was not lightly made. The debates over the use of terrorism within the FLN show that terrorism was basically a reasonable and considered political choice and that most terrorists were normal people.

Spectacular urban terrorism occurred only at specific points in the overall strategic progress of the Algerian war. In 1956, bombings were initiated in Algiers after the FLN had failed to achieve significant success with guerrilla warfare in the countryside. The FLN leaders felt that the revolution needed a political catalyst to break a basically military stalemate that would ultimately benefit the side with superior material resources— that is, the side with greater conventional power. Terrorist attacks were also timed to coincide with French government initiatives that might have threatened the FLN's position of authority with the Algerian population: for example, the holding of elections to elicit popular support for de Gaulle's "third force." At this point, the FLN did not want normal access to the French system even if it had been offered. Similarly, spectacular terrorism occurred during the final negotiations between the French government and the FLN. Paradoxical though this juxtaposition may seem in light of the FLN's evident expectation that its basic demands would be satisfied, terrorism served as a bargaining tactic at this point—a way of putting pressure on the French to reach a settlement. On the other hand, terrorism could be used by a local faction to push the central leadership either to reach a settlement without delay or to hold out for better terms. (This resembles the use of terrorism by the intransigent Palestinians to prevent compromise.) In general, terrorism of this sort escalated the conflict by broadening the scope of participation in it. By attracting widespread attention, it embarrassed the French internationally and sharpened domestic opposition to the war.

Once the FLN had acquired a certain level of compliance through the use of terrorism against Algerians, this process seemed to reach a point of diminishing returns; the continued use of compliance terrorism alone would have been unproductive, if not counterproductive. This realization may have influenced the Soummam conference in the late summer of 1956, when the FLN shifted to endorsement terrorism. Compliance and endorsement terrorism were both used from that time until the end of the war. At the transitional stage, French violence became an asset to the FLN. It created more Algerian support for the FLN than it prevented, since the vulnerability of the Algerians to the FLN, their natural sympathy for the nationalist cause, and their resentment of the French overshadowed their fear of French reprisals by that time.

Both compliance terrorism and endorsement terrorism can be interpreted as channels through which the FLN leaders communicated their own acute political discontent to the initially passive and apolitical Algerian masses. The revolutionary elite used terrorism to transmit revolutionary nationalist values to the people. Terrorism translated an unstructured and vague popular sense of grievance into explicit political rejection of the French; it stimulated awareness of injustice, polarized opinion, discouraged neutrality, and inspired a new Algerian self-confidence. Violence forced Algerians to choose sides, and it was logical that the majority, caught between the alternatives of resistance or permanent acquiescence in foreign domination, would choose revolution.

Other resistance organizations, particularly those that do not rely on rural guerrilla warfare, do not use terrorism in so extensive and complex a manner to establish a mass base. There are two possible reasons for the difference in focus. First, if a terrorist group's values and goals are not likely to be identified with by the majority of the population, neither compliance nor endorsement terrorism is likely to be useful. Minorities such as the Rote Armee Fraktion in West Germany, the Russian Narodnaya Volya of the 1870s, or the Uruguayan Tupamaros had limited potential for majority support. Such groups may believe in terrorism as the "magic means,"[5] the automatic catalyst to a mass uprising, and, unlike the FLN, they may be unwilling or unable to shift to compliance terrorism. Second, a terrorist group's potential constituency may not be accessible even if the people are genuinely sympathetic to the resistance ideology. A government may protect a population so efficiently that the terrorists cannot penetrate its security, or there may be geographical barriers. The inability of the Palestinian organizations to operate among the population of the occupied West Bank or within Israel proper (for both of the reasons just cited) was one reason for their adoption of spectacular transnational terrorism, which was a form of endorsement terrorism as well as a bid to put international pressure on Israel. Another consideration in seeking mass support is time; the mobilization of a population, through grassroots organization, propaganda, and compliance and endorsement terrorism, is a slow, arduous task without immediate payoff. If a movement needs or wants instant reward, it may turn to the international scene.

THE EFFECTIVENESS OF TERRORISM

Judging the effectiveness of terrorism requires knowledge of the ends the terrorists sought to achieve and the effects of their actions. The success or failure of terrorism depends on the discrepancy between intentions and results, and the central problem in evaluating terrorism is then one of subjectivity, since neither factor can be measured. Some terrorist goals remain private and some professed purposes are merely propagandistic. Linking changes in popular attitudes and behavior and shifts in government policies to terrorism is also a difficult task. Thus, conclusions on this subject remain tentative.

The most effective FLN terrorism took two general forms, with each in turn serving two different political purposes. The first form, endorsement terrorism, became successful after the first year of the war; by that time the FLN had launched a campaign of guerrilla warfare and the French had responded with a large-scale military effort. The primary audience for endorsement terrorism was the Algerian population, although the victims were mostly European civilians. This kind of terrorism succeeded in evoking recognition, enthusiasm, pride, and satisfaction. The same physical acts of violence—mostly urban bombings, especially the 1956–1957 events culminating in the Battle of Algiers—were also most effective in obtaining international attention (both sympathetic and hostile) for the FLN. In addition to obtaining popular endorsement and creating an image for external consumption this very successful form of terrorism often provoked indiscriminate and spontaneous counterterrorism from European civilians and the French police and military. By 1956, when the FLN had acquired a certain level of popular support, French violence often drove Algerians into the arms of the FLN. Earlier in the war, when the FLN organization was smaller, weaker, and less known, official repression was more effective, at least in the short run. As the conflict expanded, however, the French would have had to escalate repression accordingly to intimidate potential FLN sympathizers. This the Paris government was unwilling and unable to do, primarily because of domestic opposition in France. The FLN's successful provocation of counterterrorism also sparked international publicity, especially in metropolitan France. This publicity not only spread awareness of the FLN and of the gravity of the conflict, but also created an image of the FLN as the heroic underdog and of the French as brutal torturers. Only after the Battle of Algiers did the Algerian war become a perennial issue in the United Nations.

The second most effective variant of FLN terrorism was compliance terrorism, which was also used to achieve two different political ends. Terrorism was successfully directed against social and political Algerian elites to prevent the emergence of a rival contender for the allegiance of the Algerian population. These elites or potential leaders included indigenous tribal or village authorities (who, it must be noted, were not particularly powerful forces in support of the status quo, since the impact of the French conquest on Algeria's social structure had involved the destruction of local elites). These leaders were usually guilty of association with the French, but they rarely posed an overt challenge to the FLN. The MNA, on the other hand, was a deliberate rival and a threat because of its ideological kinship with the FLN. Candidates for office under de Gaulle's reform plans were also contenders for the role the FLN was determined to play. The second goal the FLN achieved through compliance terrorism against an Algerian direct audience was the isolation of the French government from the Algerian people. Terrorism cut political communication channels between regime and populace by intimidating the Algerians who would have provided essential intelligence information about the FLN to the French. This category of informers sometimes overlapped the category of existing indigenous leaders; all were collaborators with the French, and their silence, passivity, and even support of the FLN not only deprived the population of what leadership and authority structure it had, but deterred other would-be political go-betweens. The fact that political contacts were severed, however, did not mean that the economic and social ties of subservience were cut. The Algerians would not be prevented from working for French employers, although the FLN tried to do so, because economic dependence remained essential to their survival.

Several other forms of terrorism can be classified as only moderately successful, including compliance terrorism against the Algerian population as a whole to enforce obedience to FLN directions and to isolate the French. The FLN never succeeded in intimidating the entire population; its control was neither absolute nor comprehensive. Compliance tended to be transitory and dependent on the physical presence of the revolutionary organization, so that the FLN had to reestablish patterns of obedience frequently. It is difficult to evaluate the effectiveness of either organizational or factional terrorism, in which members of the FLN usually constituted the direct audience for violence against the enemy. Neither the intentions nor the consequences of revolutionary power struggles have ever become public knowledge since such an admission of disunity would have been embarrassing if not dangerous for the central leadership of the FLN.

The kinds of terrorism that met with minimal success or none at all were as varied as those that were highly or moderately successful. The

FLN could not isolate the French by intimidating Europeans who acted as links between the two communities, nor could they frighten French administrators and European civilians into leaving or compel them to accede peacefully to its desire for independence. Terrorism "to bring the war home to France" provoked an unwanted blacklash and was abandoned after the brief campaign of 1958. In addition, endorsement terrorism as a spark to ignite the conflict through a mass uprising failed completely, as the events of the Toussaint in 1954 showed.

What generalizations can be made about these rough correlations between different kinds of terrorism and the political effectiveness of each? Political power is the central aim of revolutionary terrorists; they must gain the power to challenge the regime, and their ultimate intent is to supplant the government, to "seize power" and exercise it themselves. These goals determine how terrorism is used and ultimately whether or not it is successful. Since in the early stages of the conflict it is impossible for the terrorist organization to deal directly with the government, terrorism essentially bypasses the government and puts pressure on it indirectly by affecting civilian populations. Basically, terrorism is a technique of both influence and coercion. Influence involves gaining an ascendancy over indirect audiences without visibly acting upon them. Coercion is the attempt to constrain or to compel direct audiences through the threat of force. Terrorism thus involves both persuasion and intimidation. Because the FLN sought political authority rather than merely political power—that is, because its leaders wanted the *right* to command the obedience of the Algerian people, as well as the *ability* to do so—effective influence was as important to its eventual victory as coercion.

The emotional responses to terrorism, on which the effectiveness of both influence and coercion depend, are complex. Terrorizing is by no means the most effective or the most common function of terrorism. Even the response of fear in a direct audience is only the starting point in a chain reaction. Terrorism is often effective because both the violence itself and the fear and horror it produces in the direct audience result in secondary responses in indirect audiences. The reactions of curiosity, shock, enthusiasm, or outrage were more often successful for the FLN in achieving its goals than was simple coercion through fear. For terrorism to be politically effective, it is not necessary for large numbers of people to feel afraid or threatened; indeed, it may not even be necessary to create fear at all. Indirect audiences may be stimulated merely by the spectacle of acts of violence, whatever their immediate emotional or political effect.

The case of the FLN also demonstrates the limits of compulsion. Terrorism compels only specific types of audiences to act because of the fear of personal harm. In Algeria, only the actual and potential constituency of the nationalists could be coerced into limited support. The heightened susceptibility of the Algerian audience resulted both from its acute vulnerability to terrorism and from extrinsic factors that encouraged obedience to the FLN. Ethnic affinity, ideological sympathy, distrust of the French, and the combination of compliance and endorsement terrorism after 1956 all made it more acceptable for the FLN to attack recalcitrant Algerians and more likely that fear would lead to submission rather than to revolt. On the other hand, terrorism was not successful in compelling the enemy, whether official or civilian, or distant audiences in metropolitan France, to comply with its desires. Terrorism against Europeans created little fear, but the anger it aroused in Algeria's Europeans, the attention it drew from France and the world, and the satisfaction it gave the FLN and its sympathizers were political benefits for the revolutionary movement. In sum, terrorism compels only those who are predisposed to obey; it cannot force people or governments to act against their will. It does not create loyalties, although it can reinforce preexisting allegiances.

The limits to the effectiveness of compliance terrorism may explain the shift in modern terrorism to transnational and bargaining tactics. The transference of terrorism from arenas of local conflict to the world stage may be related to the difficulties terrorists have experienced in coercing their governmental antagonists. In cases where conflict involved a colonial government, metropolitan authorities and populations could be persuaded to make concessions at the expense of the settler community; Vietnam and Ulster may be interpreted as neocolonial situations in this respect. Today, however, most terrorists must confront intransigent governments directly, and they often demand solutions that governments cannot offer—for example, the creation of a Palestinian state in what is now Israel. Faced with such an impasse, the terrorists can appeal to world opinion and sympathetic third parties to put pressure on the recalcitrant government, or they can seize hostages to extort specific concessions.

The government, in its response to terrorism, encounters similar problems of coercing support. Official repression such as reprisals against civilians or torture and unofficial counterterror may backfire. Repression that is not severe enough to crush all opposition may intimidate some of the people but drive others to support an attractive alternative authority. Where there is no acceptable substitute for the incumbent government, intimidation may be more effective. Yet authoritarian methods, especially inefficient ones, create a bad press, and democratic governments can be gravely embarrassed by such affronts to their reputations.

Two general factors deserve emphasis as explanations of the overall effectiveness of FLN terrorism. One concerns the FLN's use of terrorism, the other the French response. This study has pointed out that a preoccupation with eventual legitimacy—with acceptability as an appropriate government by the Algerian people, by the French, and by foreign states—colored the FLN's use of terrorism. Although the FLN began as a small band of would-be revolutionaries, the organization possessed from the outset a high potential for popular support and for respectability. This potential for legitimacy was related to the revolutionary conditions that permitted terrorism and the FLN ideology; essentially, the *chefs historiques* of the revolution chose the right goals at the right time.

Not only were the objective conditions auspicious, but the leaders of the FLN used discrimination and care in their terrorist strategy because of their need for legitimacy. The distinctions they made among different audiences, the effort they expended to control terrorism and preserve the organization's internal unity, their concern with the image the FLN projected abroad, their sensitivity to the responses to terrorism, their avoidance of accidental victims, and their verbal strategy of ideological and emotional justification for terrorism—all of these were results of their search for political legitimacy. Groups that are not concerned with their future political status, that have no hope of becoming viable governments, are not likely to be this discriminating in their employment of violence. In Algeria, for example, the OAS was not as disciplined, not as attentive to the selection of victims, and not as sensitive to adverse reactions as the FLN. The OAS was part of a military-colon revolt, but its aims were reactionary rather than revolutionary; it wanted to change the Algerian policy of the French government, not to overturn the entire French social and political system and substitute a new order. (The Provisional IRA has suffered from the same limitations; doomed to be permanent outcasts even if their goal of a united Ireland is reached, its leaders are not concerned with gaining the status of a legitimate political opponent.)

The French response to FLN terrorism, on the other hand, failed dismally because it reinforced the FLN's legitimacy while undermining that of the French government. By treating terrorism as a military rather than a political problem, French leaders neglected the impact of their policies on the Algerian population and on the French army, with grave consequences for civilian rule in France. The violent response to terrorism aided the FLN in politicizing and mobilizing the population. Circumstances limited the choices of the French, however, hampering the government's ability to respond effectively while aiding the revolutionaries. The government never possessed the loyalty of the Algerian population, the obedience of the European community was shallow rooted, and colonial authority was tenuous from the start. The history of colonial coercion and illegality simplified the FLN's task of justifying terrorism, and the government's repetition of unimaginative tactics of repression was both inevitable and self-defeating. The French response underscored rather than erased audience distinctions, and the regime's emphasis on offensive strategy failed to protect the most vulnerable victims of terrorism. The Algiers bombings of 1956 were unanticipated, and it took even highly trained professional troops more than nine months to destroy the FLN's terrorist cells. In the end, the violence of the French response increased publicity for the war and for the FLN's cause. A weak and divided Fourth Republic bowed to pressure from European colonialists and the military, and the mistakes committed during the period 1954–1958 could not be rectified by de Gaulle, who had to reestablish the political authority and stability of the central government before embarking on reforms in Algeria. By the time cautious changes in policy could be introduced, it was too late to go back.

The Algerian case demonstrates that one of the most serious results of antigovernmental terrorism in general is undisciplined counterterrorism by civilians, which is often condoned if not aided by the government. In Algeria, the OAS was a greater threat to the stability of the French government than it was to the survival of the FLN. There are many other examples of this phenomenon of parallel reaction, particularly in Latin America. In Guatemala, Brazil, and Argentina, right-wing terrorism has succeeded leftist terrorism. Even military dictatorships find it difficult to reestablish control in such cases. The government's authority is undermined at home and its international reputation is diminished. Political control of violence is as necessary for an efficient government response as it is for effective revolutionary terrorism.

It is often said that terrorism thrives on publicity, and that without the instantaneous attention that is focused on present-day terrorist exploits by the press, terrorism, unheeded and thus unrewarded, would subside. Publicity is cited as a necessary condition for the wave of transnational terrorism of the 1960s and 1970s, but the relationship between publicity and effectiveness was not so definitive in the case of FLN terrorism. In general, the terrorism of the FLN was most significant in its impact on the masses of Algeria, most of whom were illiterate and did not own television sets or radios or read Western newspapers (which were often censored). Even in urban areas, most Algerians probably learned about terrorism through personal experience, word of mouth, and FLN propaganda. This is not to deny that communication of the threat inherent in the act of terrorism is not crucial to the process, nor that publicity for transnational terrorism is not critical, but publicity is not always essential for effective terrorism. Publicity is central to the process of influencing audiences who are physically distant from the scene of the conflict, and in cases where these audiences are foremost in the terrorist strategy, terrorists turn to the cruelly spectacular acts of violence that impress at long range.

The final criterion for judging the effectiveness of FLN terrorism is the question of whether terrorism was necessary to the FLN's ultimate victory over the French. That answer depends on an assessment of why Algeria became independent. In the end, it was not so much that the FLN "won" but that the French "lost" the war. Eight years of struggle exhausted the French politically if not materially. The war became intolerable to a metropolitan population that had allowed decisions about Algeria to be dictated by the colon lobby while those choices cost France nothing. The colons' loss of control over decisions in Paris meant that a new set of national interests came into play, and that the preservation of Algérie française was no longer first in the order of priorities. The need to fight a prolonged and unheroic war in Algeria raised the cost of following a colonial policy. The cost of staying on finally surpassed that of withdrawing. Once the conflict was fully engaged, the FLN's major task was to maintain popular awareness of its existence. Whereas the French had to win, the FLN only had to avoid losing. This was possible because the FLN managed to acquire the support of the Algerian people and to keep the issue of Algerian independence alive in France and abroad. Support for the nationalist cause was in part a reaction to colonialism. There was no reason for the Algerian masses to feel loyalty to their French rulers, and the FLN was a much more appealing subject for identification on ethnic, religious, and cultural grounds. In addition, to most Algerians, an unknowable future under the FLN was preferable to the colonial past they knew.[6]

If metropolitan public opinion was indeed the key to the outcome of the war, then the importance of FLN terrorism lay in its influence on French politics. Terrorism played a major role as a constant reminder of the presence of the FLN, creating enough disorder in rural areas to require a French effort to maintain order and enough commotion in the cities to spark European unrest, military repression, and extensive publicity. Terrorism was also critical to the FLN's bid for the allegiance and the obedience of the Algerian people. The FLN could not have gained a foothold for the rural organization after its opening move in 1954 without the use of compliance terrorism against Algerians. It would not have made the leap to international prominence in 1956–1957, which led to increased foreign assistance, the attention of metropolitan France, and the establishment of a provisional Algerian government, without the Battle of Algiers. Urban terrorism was also an important factor in obtaining the endorsement of Algerians and provoking a military revolt in 1958 that resulted in de Gaulle's return to power. The FLN used terrorism to keep the revolution politically alive through the French military successes of 1959 and after, which almost obliterated the rural guerrilla networks.

However, one should not conclude that terrorism by itself would have been sufficient for a nationalist victory. The resort to terrorism does not guarantee success. For the FLN, the real grievances against French colonialism; the determination, preoccupation with legitimacy, skilful organization of populations, and propaganda and diplomatic efforts of the FLN leadership; the magnetic attraction of nationalism; a terrain that favored guerrilla warfare (including the availability of sanctuaries across Algeria's borders); and the blunders of French policy were also important determinants in the outcome. It is impossible to separate one factor from the composite in order to weigh it and compare it to other means. To place a value on the political utility of terrorism per se, without considering its context, would be unrealistic. Violence is essential to the confrontation politics of national liberation, but terrorism as the unique means of resistance can succeed only in rare circumstances. This lesson should be a comfort to governments that are threatened by terrorism and a warning to aspiring revolutionaries, who ignore it at their peril.

Notes

INTRODUCTION

1. Several works cover a broad historical range of incidents of terrorism. The best are Paul Wilkinson, *Political Terrorism* (New York: John Wiley and Sons, 1974) and Walter Laqueur, *Terrorism* (London: Weidenfeld and Nicolson, 1977); see also Roland Gaucher, *Les Terroristes* (Paris: Albin-Michel, 1965).

2. The United States government has identified more than fifty "noteworthy practitioners" of transnational terrorism in the period 1965–1975. See David L. Milbank, *International and Transnational Terrorism: Diagnosis and Prognosis* (Washington, D.C.: Central Intelligence Agency, 1976).

CHAPTER I

1. See Eric R. Wolf, *Peasant Wars of the Twentieth Century* (New York: Harper & Row, 1969), pp. 222–24, and John Dunn, *Modern Revolutions: An Introduction to the Analysis of a Political Phenomenon* (Cambridge: Cambridge University Press, 1972), p. 154.

2. The native population of Algeria, a heterogeneous ethnic group of various tribal federations speaking Berber dialects, was converted to Islam by Arab conquerors during the seventh to twelfth centuries A.D. Thus the twentieth-century population contained both Arabs and Islamized "Berbers," who were located, significantly, in the mountainous regions of Kabylia and the Aurès Mountains.

3. Charles-André Julien, *L'Afrique du Nord en marche: Nationalismes musulmans et souveraineté française*, 3rd ed. (Paris: Julliard, 1972), p. 97.

4. Ibid., p. 251.

5. See Yves Courrière, *La guerre d'Algérie*, vol. 1: *Les fils de la Toussaint* (Paris: Fayard, 1968), pp. 40–46.

6. Julien, *L'Afrique du Nord*, p. 284.

7. William B. Quandt, *Revolution and Political Leadership: Algeria, 1954– 1968* (Cambridge: The M.I.T. Press, 1969).

8. Ibid., p. 68.

9. Ibid., p. 79.

10. Ibid., p. 107.

11. For a description of the FLN/ALN organization, see Alf Andrew Heggoy, *Insurgency and Counterinsurgency in Algeria* (Bloomington: Indiana University Press, 1972), pp. 107—29.

12. Colonel Yves Godard, *Les paras dans la ville* (Paris: Fayard, 1972), p. 370.

13. For further details of the bomb network see Godard, *Les paras*, p. 334, and General Jacques Massu, *La vraie bataille d'Alger* (Paris: Plon, 1971), pp. 381—92.

14. See Quandt, *Revolution and Political Leadership*, pp. 165—66.

15. *Le Monde*, Oct. 31, 1957, and Jan. 21, 1958.

16. The FFFLN furnished 60 percent of the budget for the interior, more than any foreign contributor; see Tayeb Belloula, *Les Algériens en France* (Alger: Editions nationales algériennes, 1965), p. 99.

17. On May 1, 1958, the French reported that the ALN had lost twelve thousand men in the past four months and that only one-fifth of their arms shipments had passed through successfully. Courrière, *La guerre d'Algérie*, vol. 3: *L'heure des colonels* (Paris: Fayard, 1970), p. 244.

18. Courrière, in *La guerre d'Algérie*, Vol. 4: *Les feux du désespoir: (La fin d'un empire)* (Paris: Fayard, 1971), pp. 229—35, describes the early development of the OAS. The most detailed account is Morland, Barangé, and Martinez (pseudonyms of police officers), *Histoire de l'organisation de l'Armée Secrète* (Paris: Julliard, 1964). An interesting collection of documents is *OAS parle* (Paris: Julliard, 1964). Paul Henissart, *Wolves in the City* (London: Rupert Hart-Davis, 1971) is a significant English work on the subject.

19. An excellent account of the FLN-OAS negotiations is Fernand Carréras, *L'accord F.L.N.-O.A.S., des négotiations secrètes au cessez-le-feu* (Paris: R. Laffont, 1967). By 1971, only thirteen hundred Europeans had asked for Algerian citizenship; see *Le Monde*, June 17, 1971, p. 7.

CHAPTER II

1. See Eugene Victor Walter, *Terror and Resistance: A Study of Political Violence* (New York: Oxford University Press, 1969), and Alexander Dallin and George W. Breslauer, *Political Terror in Communist Systems* (Stanford: Stanford University Press, 1970).

2. Walter, *Terror and Resistance*, pp. 7—8.

3. See Jerzy Waciorski, *Le terrorisme politique* (Paris: A Pedone, 1939), who noted the etymological derivation of the term. Thomas P. Thornton, in "Terror as a Weapon of Political Agitation," in *Internal War: Problems and Approaches*, ed. Harry Eckstein (New York: Free Press, 1964), pp. 71—72, uses "terror" to refer to the "tool" that produces the emotional condition.

4. Thornton, "Terror as a Weapon," p. 76.

5. The occurrence of some act of terrorism at some time in some place, however, may be *generally*, but not *specifically*, predictable under circumstances of sustained violence.

6. See Hanna F. Pitkin, *The Concept of Representation* (Berkeley: University of California Press, 1972).

7. Cf. Thornton, "Terror as a Weapon," pp. 77—78.

8. Murray Clark Havens, Carl Leiden, and Karl M. Schmitt, *The Politics of Assassination* (Englewood Cliffs, N.J.: Prentice-Hall, Inc., 1970), p. 3.

9. Jean-Marc Théollèyre, *Ces procès qui ébranlèrent la France* (Paris: B. Grasset, 1966), p. 127.

10. Cf. Thornton, "Terror as a Weapon," p. 79. A "direct audience" is comparable to Thornton's "identification group."

11. Roger le Tourneau, *Evolution politique de l'Afrique du Nord musulmane: 1920—1961* (Paris: Armand Colin, 1962), p. 405, quoted in Alf Andrew Heggoy, *Insurgency and Counterinsurgency in Algeria* (Bloomington: Indiana University Press, 1972), p. 156.

12. For example, *El Moudjahid* and *Résistance Algérienne* were regular publications (in French) that carried explicit accounts of specific acts of violence.

13. Pierre Bourdieu, "The Sentiment of Honour in Kabyle Society," in *Honour and Shame: The Values of Mediterranean Society*, ed. J. G. Peristiany (London: Weidenfeld and Nicolson, 1965), pp. 201—03. See also his *Sociologie de l'Algérie*, 3rd ed., Collection "Que sais-je" (Paris: Presses universitaires de France, 1970), translated as *The Algerians* (Boston: Beacon Press, 1962).

14. Ernest Gellner, "The Unknown Apollo of Biskra: The Social Base of Algerian Puritanism," *Government and Opposition* 9, no. 3 (Summer 1974): 287—88.

15. Omar Chaïr, "Des musulmans si tranquilles," *Historia Magazine*, no. 195 (n.d.): 59.

16. See Yves Godard, *Les paras dans la ville* (Paris: Fayard, 1972), p. 354.

17. Amar Ouzegane, *Le meilleur combat* (Paris: Julliard, 1962), p. 257. Thornton, in "Terror as a Weapon," p. 76, holds that "the insurgent must attempt to communicate effectively to his audience the idea that terror is the only weapon appropriate to the situation."

18. See Jacques Massu, *La vraie bataille d'Alger* (Paris: Plon, 1971), p. 120.

19. See, for example, Peter Paret, *French Revolutionary Warfare from Indochina to Algeria* (London: Pall Mall Press, 1964), pp. 12—15; or John H. McCuen, *The Art of Counter-Revolutionary War* (Harrisburg, Pa.: Stackpole Books, 1966), pp. 30—40.

20. Freida Fromm-Reichmann, "Psychiatric Aspects of Anxiety," in *Identity and Anxiety: Survival of the Person in Mass Society*, ed. Maurice R. Stein, Arthur J. Vidich, and David Manning White (New York: Free Press, 1960), p. 130; and Irving L. Janis, "Psychological Effects of Warnings," *Man and Society in Disaster*, ed. George W. Baker and Dwight W. Chapman (New York: Basic Books, 1962), p. 59.

21. David C. Rapoport, *Assassination and Terrorism* (Toronto: Canadian Broadcasting Corporation, 1971), p. 44.

22. Irving L. Janis, *Air War and Emotional Stress: Psychological Studies of Bombing and Civilian Defense* (New York: McGraw-Hill, 1951), pp. 23—24 and 173—74.

23. See especially Bruno Bettelheim, *The Informed Heart* (New York: Free Press, 1960); and Hilde O. Bluhm, "How Did They Survive? Mechanisms of Defense in Nazi Concentration Camps," and Eugene Kogon, "Daily Routine in

Buchenwald," in *Mass Society in Crisis*, eds. Bernard Rosenberg et al. (New York: Macmillan, 1964).

24. Kurt Riezler, "The Social Psychology of Fear," in Stein, *Identity and Anxiety*, p. 152.

25. Chalmers Johnson, *Revolutionary Change* (Boston: Little, Brown, 1966), p. 8. The disappearance of community solidarity is also characteristic of panic:

> Panic, rather than being antisocial, is non-social behavior; ordinary social relationships are disregarded and pre-existent group action patterns fail to be applied. This disintegration of social norms and cessation of action with reference to a group or institutional pattern sometimes results in the shattering of the strongest primary group ties and the ignoring of the most expected behavior patterns.

(Enrico L. Quarantelli, "The Nature and Conditions of Panic," in *Panic Behavior*, ed. Duane P. Schultz [New York: Random House, 1964], p. 41).

26. Mouloud Feraoun, *Journal 1955–1962* (Paris: Seuil, 1962), pp. 96–97, 109, 170, and 160 (respectively).

27. Jacques Soustelle, *Aimée et souffrante Algérie* (Paris: Plon, 1956), pp. 121–24.

28. Fromm-Reichmann, "Psychiatric Aspects of Anxiety," p. 130.

29. Joost A. M. Meerloo, "Brainwashing and Menticide," in Stein, *Identity and Anxiety*, p. 513.

30. The "Document on Terror" is nominally a Communist instruction manual for the subversion of Eastern Europe, but its authenticity is doubtful. See *News from behind the Iron Curtain* (a publication of the National Committee for a Free Europe) 1, no. 13 (March 1952): 44–57.

31. Ibid., pp. 45–46.

32. Ibid., pp. 46–47.

33. Ibid., pp. 49–50 and 53.

34. Ibid., p. 51.

35. Feraoun, *Journal*, p. 203.

36. See Howard Leventhal et al., "Effects of Fear and Specificity of Recommendation upon Attitudes and Behavior," *Journal of Personality and Social Psychology* 2, no. 1 (July 1965): 20–29.

37. Feraoun, *Journal*, pp. 58 and 134.

38. Ted Robert Gurr, "Psychological Factors in Civil Violence," *World Politics* 20, no. 2 (Jan. 1968): 247–51, and Leonard Berkowitz, *Aggression: A Social Psychological Analysis* (New York: McGraw-Hill, 1962). A persuasive rebuttal of the frustration-aggression hypothesis is Peter A. Lupsha, "Explanation of Political Violence: Some Psychological Theories versus Indignation," *Politics and Society* 2, no. 1 (Fall 1971): 89–104.

39. Berkowitz, *Aggression*, p. 118.

40. Ibid., pp. 119 and 130–31.

41. Yacef, head of the ZAA, even ordered bomb explosions in retaliation; see Mohamed Lebjaoui, *Vérités sur la Révolution algérienne* (Paris: Gallimard,

1970), p. 242, and Massu, *La vraie bataille d' Alger*, p. 306, quoting from the military interrogation of Yacef after his arrest.

42. Ted Robert Gurr, *Why Men Rebel* (Princeton: Princeton University Press, 1970), p. 213.

43. Nathan Leites and Charles Wolf, Jr., *Rebellion and Authority: An Analytic Essay on Insurgent Conflicts* (Chicago: Markham Publishing Co., 1970), p. 10.

44. Feraoun, *Journal*, p. 47.

45. Germaine Tillion, *Les ennemis complémentaires* (Paris: Minuit, 1960), pp. 176–77.

46. Ibid., pp. 49–50.

47. Ibid., pp. 52–53.

48. Frantz Fanon, *The Wretched of the Earth* (London: MacGibbon & Kee, 1965), p. 73.

49. Ouzegane, *Le meilleur combat*, p. 261.

50. Fanon, *Wretched of the Earth*, p. 67.

51. Philippe Ivernel, "Violence d'hier et d'aujourd'hui," *Esprit* 30, no. 10 (Oct. 1962): 392–93.

52. Ouzegane, *Le meilleur combat*, p. 257.

53. General Massu (*La vraie bataille d'Alger*, pp. 30 and 152) even complained that the government allowed too many such sensitive officials to remain in positions of authority in Algeria; he claimed that they impaired the efficiency of the army and the police. Paul Teitgen, the head of the Algiers police during the Battle of Algiers, responded by suing Massu for slander (see *Le Monde*, Mar. 9, 1972, p. 11).

54. Irving L. Janis and Daniel Katz, "The Reduction of Intergroup Hostility," *Journal of Conflict Resolution* 3, no. 1 (March 1959): 91–93.

55. Franz Neumann, "Anxiety and Politics," in Stein, *Identity and Anxiety*, pp. 288–89.

56. Tillion, *Les ennemis*, p. 47.

57. Interview with G. Tillion. Cf. Saadi Yacef, *Souvenirs de la bataille d'Alger* (Paris: Julliard, 1962). Colonel Godard (*Les paras*, p. 344), however, reported that Yacef bragged about the "carnage" his bombs caused.

58. Interview with G. Tillion; see also Massu, *La vraie bataille d'Alger*, pp. 183–91.

59. Massu, *La vraie bataille d'Alger*, pp. 181–82; see also the account of Taleb's trial in *Le Monde*, Dec. 7, 1957, p. 2 (he was executed).

60. See her memoirs (Zohra Drif, *La mort de mes frères* [Paris, Maspéro, 1960]); the participation of so many Algériennes in FLN terrorism is especially interesting in light of Irving Horowitz's proposition that "for the most part terrorism is a male activity" (Irving Louis Horowitz, "Political Terrorism and State Power," *Journal of Political and Military Sociology* 1 [Spring 1973]: 148).

61. Thomas P. Thornton, "Terror as a Weapon of Political Agitation," in *Internal War: Problems and Approaches*, ed. Harry Eckstein (New York: Free Press, 1964), p. 83 (see further pp. 78–88).

62. Ibid., p. 82.

CHAPTER III

1. The text of the declaration is reproduced in Yves Courrière, *La guerre d'Algérie*, vol. 1: *Les fils de la Toussaint*. (Paris: Fayard, 1968), pp. 443–46.

2. Ibid., pp. 202 and 254.

3. Arslan Humbaraci, *Algeria: A Revolution that Failed* (New York: Praeger, 1966), p. 33, recounts that he was told the revolution was begun with less than fifty obsolete shotguns, and that this was certainly not far from the truth.

4. Mohamed Lebjaoui, *Vérités sur la révolution algérienne* (Paris: Gallimard, 1970), p. 29. See also William Quandt, *Revolution and Political Leadership: Algeria, 1954–1968* (Cambridge: The M.I.T. Press, 1969), pp. 93–94, who noted the FLN's disappointment with the ambiguity of the mass response. He also considered the elimination of the MTLD by suspicious French police a subsidiary aim, one the FLN did achieve.

5. Général C. R. Cherrière, "Les débuts de l'insurrection algérienne," *Revue de défense nationale* 23 (Dec. 1956): 1453.

6. Germaine Tillion, however, who was in the Aurès from December 1954, to April 1955, reported that the population was "aghast" at the November 1 events, and that one of the FLN's first propaganda efforts was to dissociate itself from the death of Guy Monnerot. *Les ennemis complémentaires* (Paris: Minuit, 1960), pp. 166–67.

7. Courrière, *La guerre d'Algérie*, vol. 2: *Le temps des léopards* (Paris: Fayard, 1969), p. 172.

8. Ibid., pp. 373–76.

9. Therefore this group also figured prominently in terrorist acts that were designed to isolate the French.

10. See Eugène Mannoni, "M. N. A. et F. L. N. se disputent sans merci le monopole du nationalisme," *Le Monde*, Oct. 17, 1956, p. 5, and "Document: Le terrorisme algérien dans le Nord," *Esprit* 29, no. 10 (Oct. 1961): 488–94.

11. The FLN also supplanted the gangster underworld that had previously ruled the Algiers Casbah. The Parti Communiste Algérien (PCA), a potential rival, very soon gave in to the FLN; after a short-lived attempt at independent resistance, most of its twelve thousand members, the majority of them European, joined the FLN individually.

12. Those who broke FLN rules not only were physically mutilated but also were subject to the general opprobrium of the population, according to Albert-Paul Lentin, *Le dernier quart d'heure* (Paris: Julliard, 1963), p. 119. This covers the period 1960–1962.

13. See "*Le Monde* et les moutons," in *Résistance Algérienne*, no. 29–30 (May 11–20, 1957): 4, which criticizes *Le Monde* for accepting a defamatory version of an attack—that a pharmacist was assassinated because he had failed to pay his monthly dues to the FLN. The author of the article was angry because French journals had failed to print a letter correcting their accounts.

14. Youssef Zertouti, "Chefs de la Wilaya 2," *Historia Magazine*, no. 206 (n.d.): 402–03.

15. Figures reported in *Le Monde*, September 2, 1955, p. 2.

16. Courrière, *La guerre d'Algérie*, vol. 2, p. 187; see especially pp. 173–87.

17. Quandt, *Revolution and Political Leadership*, pp. 94—97.

18. Ibid., p. 98.

19. Courrière, *La guerre d'Algérie*, vol. 2, pp. 201—02 and 246.

20. See the FLN statement "The Saboteurs of Our Struggle," included in Colette and Francis Jeanson, *L'Algérie hors la loi* (Paris: Seuil, 1955), p. 308.

21. See, for example, the account of an interview with Zohra Drif in Quandt, *Revolution and Political Leadership*, p. 94.

22. Jean Jacques Susini puts the number of Algerian victims at approximately four hundred; see his article "La mort du maire de Boufarik," *Historia Magazine*, no. 221 (n.d.): 869.

23. France, Service de l'Information du Cabinet du Ministre Résidant en Algérie, *Programme et action du gouvernement en Algérie. Mesures de pacification et réformes.* (Alger: Imprimerie officielle du Gouvernement Général de l'Algérie, 1956), pp. 17—19.

24. Jacques Soustelle, *Aimée et souffrante Algérie* (Paris: Plon, 1956), especially p. 121.

25. See, for example, Jean-Jacques Servan-Schreiber, *Lieutenant en Algérie* (Paris: Julliard, 1957), especially pp. 94—95. Also Michel Déon, *L'armée d'Algérie et la pacification* (Paris: Plon, 1959), pp. 18—19.

26. Nathan Leites and Charles Wolf, Jr., *Rebellion and Authority: An Analytic Essay on Insurgent Conflicts* (Chicago: Markham Publishing Co., 1970), pp. 55 and 152.

27. Tillion, *Les ennemis complémentaires*, pp. 176—77; also Courrière, *La guerre d'Algérie*, vol. 2, pp. 397—401.

28. Mohamed Lebjaoui, *Bataille d'Alger ou bataille d'Algérie?* (Paris: Gallimard, 1972), p. 18.

29. Ibid., pp. 18—19.

30. Courrière, *La guerre d'Algérie*, vol. 4: *Les feux du désespoir* (Paris: Fayard, 1971), pp. 620—24.

31. Ibid., pp. 624—33.

32. "Ceci s'est passé à Koléa," *Résistance Algérienne*, no. 23 (March 1—10, 1957): 5.

33. Abdelkader Rahmani, *L'affaire des officiers algériens* (Paris: Seuil, 1959), p. 53.

34. "Notre guerre de libération sera victorieuse," *El Moudjahid*, no. 23 (May 5, 1958): 1 and 3.

35. See Pierre Bourdieu's eloquent description of "The Revolution Within the Revolution," in his book *The Algerians* (Boston: Beacon Press, 1962), pp. 145—92. This chapter was added for the English edition of *Sociologie de l'Algérie* (3rd ed., Collection "Que sais-je," [Paris: Presses universitaires de France, 1970]).

CHAPTER IV

1. The issue of attacking European civilians will be discussed under the topic of terrorism designed to influence external audiences, since it was pri-

marily for this purpose—the publicity value of spectacular urban terrorism—that the FLN leadership made the decision to use this strategy.

2. See further Alf Andrew Heggoy, *Insurgency and Counterinsurgency in Algeria* (Bloomington: Indiana University Press, 1972), especially Chapter 7, "Some Motives for Support of the FLN-ALN," pp. 130–40.

3. See Jean Servier, *Adieu djebels* (Paris: France-Empire, 1958). Servier, an ethnologist, noted that before the revolution most of the land in Algeria was held by large landowners. When the French administration undertook "timid" agricultural reforms, the land was divided up into parcels, each "given solemnly to a Muslim who thus found himself simultaneously condemned to death. A few days later, a patrol found the body of the happy proprietor, his throat cut, in his field" (p. 200). Servier thought that the land should have been distributed to villages as communal property, following traditional custom, rather than to individuals whom the FLN could easily single out as targets.

4. J. C. Guillebaud, "Les harkis oubliés par l'histoire," *Le Monde*, July 3, 1973, p. 9.

5. For example, Colonel Roger Trinquier testified during General Salan's trial that after the 1958 referendum on the constitution of the Fifth Republic, the army seized the FLN archives for a small village, which showed that fifty-eight peasants had been killed because they had voted. *Le procès du général Raoul Salan: Stenographie complète des audiences—requisitiore—plaidoiries—verdict.* (Paris: Nouvelles éditions latines, 1962), p. 361.

6. See Michael K. Clark, *Algeria in Turmoil* (New York: Grosset and Dunlap, 1960), pp. 188–99.

7. Unfortunately, these people also became the victims of OAS terrorism. Then it became almost impossible to identify the authors of attacks, whether FLN or OAS. The significance of acts was thus obscured.

8. France, Service de l'Information du Cabinet du Ministre Résidant en Algérie, *Programme et action du gouvernement en Algérie. Mesures de pacification et reformes.* (Alger: Imprimerie officielle du Gouvernement Général de l'Algérie, 1956), pp. 17–19.

9. Yves Courrière, *La guerre d'Algérie*, vol. 2: *Le temps des léopards* (Paris: Fayard, 1969), p. 246.

10. Colonel Yves Godard, *Les paras dans la ville* (Paris: Fayard, 1972), p. 102.

11. Letter from a "Political Commissioner of the ALN," supposedly Amar Ouamrane, in *France-Observateur*, Oct. 13, 1955.

12. *Le Figaro*, June 19, 1961, p. 6. The period averaged thirty-seven incidents of terrorism per day; 152 Algerians were killed by the FLN.

13. "Le FIDAI: Sentinelle avancée de la révolution," *El Moudjahid*, no. 9 (Aug. 20, 1957): 3.

14. Godard, *Les paras*, pp. 353–54.

15. "Le FIDAI," p. 3.

16. *Combat*, June 23, 1958.

17. "Le FIDAI," p. 3.

18. Mouloud Feraoun, *Journal, 1955–1962* (Paris: Seuil, 1962), pp. 94–95. Entry dated March 12, 1956.

CHAPTER V

1. Thomas P. Thornton, "Terror as a Weapon of Political Agitation," in *Internal War: Problems and Approaches,* ed. Harry Eckstein (New York: Free Press, 1964), p. 82.

2. Roger Trinquier, *Modern Warfare: A French View of Counterinsurgency* (New York: Praeger, 1964), pp. 14—15.

3. This is the version of the film *La Bataille d'Alger* that Yacef directed; see also Yves Courrière, "La Casbah de Yacef Saadi," *Historia Magazine,* no. 208 (n.d.): 462—67.

4. Jacques Massu, *La vraie bataille d'Alger* (Paris: Plon, 1971), p. 124.

5. Germaine Tillion, *Les ennemis complémentaires* (Paris: Minuit, 1960), p. 205.

6. See Albert-Paul Lentin, *Le dernier quart d'heure* (Paris: Julliard, 1963), pp. 123—24.

7. Eugene Victor Walter, *Terror and Resistance: A Study of Political Violence* (New York: Oxford University Press, 1969), p. 25.

8. Ibid., p. 26.

9. Peter Braestrup, "Partisan Tactics—Algerian Style," in *Modern Guerrilla Warfare,* ed. Franklin M. Osanka (New York: Free Press, 1962), p. 382.

10. See *Le Monde,* Oct. 7, 1959, p. 2.

11. Yves Courrière, *La guerre d'Algérie,* vol. 4: *Les feux du désespoir* (Paris: Fayard, 1971), pp. 79—110; see also Charles de Gaulle, *Mémoires d'espoir: Le renouveau 1958—1962* (Paris: Plon, 1970), pp. 104—05, and Lentin, *Le dernier quart d'heure,* pp. 228—33.

12. See Courrière, *La guerre d'Algérie,* vol. 3: *L'heure des colonels* (Paris: Fayard, 1970), pp. 132—60 and 419—24. The French discovered mass graves containing four hundred bodies in 1958; see *Le Monde,* Sept. 24, 1958, p. 2.

13. Mohamed Lebjaoui, *Vérités sur la révolution algérienne* (Paris: Gallimard, 1970), p. 243.

14. William B. Quandt, *Revolution and Political Leadership: Algeria, 1954—1968* (Cambridge: The M.I.T. Press, 1969), p. 142.

15. See Thomas C. Schelling, *The Strategy of Conflict* (New York: Oxford University Press, 1963), pp. 18—19.

16. In the fall of 1959, de Gaulle proposed negotiations, but the FLN spurned his offer by naming as negotiators the FLN leaders who had been imprisoned after their plane was seized by the French in 1956. Talks finally opened at Melun in June 1960.

17. It was this wave of terrorism in the winter of 1959—1960 that led to the Barricades Affair.

18. Courrière, *La guerre d'Algérie,* vol. 4, p. 31.

19. Text of the speech in *Combat,* Feb. 18, 1960.

20. *El Moudjahid,* no. 24 (May 29, 1958): 1.

21. See Courrière, *La guerre d'Algérie,* vol. 3, pp. 173—92. Mohamed Lebjaoui, for example, stated: "Like any revolution, unfortunately, ours had its somber pages. Because of its political consequences, that of the assassination of Abane was the blackest." (Mohamed Lebjaoui, *Vérités sur la révolution algérienne,* p. 242).

CHAPTER VI

1. James N. Rosenau, "Internal War as an International Event," in *International Aspects of Civil Strife*, ed. James N. Rosenau (Princeton: Princeton University Press, 1964), pp. 50—59.

2. Robert Jervis, *The Logic of Images in International Relations* (Princeton: Princeton University Press, 1970), p. 6.

3. See Andrew J. R. Mack, "Why Big Nations Lose Small Wars: The Politics of Asymmetrical Conflict," *World Politics* 27, no. 2 (Jan. 1975): 175—200.

4. Yves Courrière, *La guerre d'Algérie*, vol. 2: *Le temps des léopards* (Paris: Fayard, 1969), pp. 394—95.

5. *Résistance algérienne*, no. 17 (Jan. 1, 1957): 1. The issue had first been raised in 1955, but France had successfully blocked attempts to put it on the agenda. See Mohamed Alwan, *Algeria before the UN* (New York: Robert Speller and Sons, 1959).

6. See Colonel Yves Godard, *Les paras dans la ville* (Paris: Fayard, 1972), p. 355. He cites Yacef on this point.

7. Robert Gauthier, "Septième Anniversaire," *Le Monde*, Nov. 2, 1961, p. 3, expressed the view that "more than to the cowardliness of the [terrorist] attacks, international opinion was sensitive to the brutality of the repressive methods largely applied since 1956. . . ."

8. Edward Behr, *The Algerian Problem* (London: Hodder and Stoughton, 1961), p. 115.

9. The text of Pineau's speech can be found in France, La Documentation française, *Textes du jour*, No. 0.466, Feb. 7, 1957. See also *Le Monde*, Feb. 8, 1957, pp. 1 and 3, in whose opinion the speech elicited much support for the French case, especially from the United States.

10. See *Le Monde*, May 21, 1959, p. 4.

11. Mohamed Lebjaoui, *Vérités sur la révolution algérienne* (Paris: Gallimard, 1970), p. 77.

12. Ibid., p. 82.

13. Ibid., pp. 82—83.

14. William Quandt, *Revolution and Political Leadership: Algeria, 1954—1968* (Cambridge: The M.I.T. Press, 1969), pp. 115—23.

15. *El Moudjahid*, no. 29 (Sept. 17, 1958): 9. Ferhat Abbas later said that the decision had been made immediately after May 13 (*Le Monde*, Aug. 28, 1958, p. 3).

16. *El Moudjahid*, p. 9.

17. Ibid.

18. Ibid.

19. *Le Monde*, Aug. 28, 1958, p. 3.

20. Front de Libération Nationale, Fédération de France, ed., *F.L.N. Documents à l'adresse du peuple français*, no. 1 (Jan. 1959): 8 and 10—11.

21. Interview with Arthur Rosenberg of *Der Tag*, quoted in *Le Monde*, Oct. 15, 1958, p. 2.

22. Jacques C. Duchemin, *Histoire du F.L.N.* (Paris: La Table Ronde, 1962), p. 297.

23. Yves Courrière, *La guerre d'Algérie*, vol. 3: *L'heure des colonels* (Paris: Fayard, 1970), pp. 408–09.

24. Philippe Herreman, "La tendance intransigéante se renforce au sein du F.L.N.," *Le Monde*, Jan. 4, 1958, pp. 1 and 3, and "Le F.L.N. semble considerer toujours le général de Gaulle comme le Français le mieux placé pour mettre fin au conflit," *Le Monde*, Dec. 20, 1958, p. 6.

25. *Le Monde*, Oct. 11, 1958, p. 4.

26. From 1956 to 1960, only 20 French policemen and 67 civilians were killed; most of the civilian deaths were accidental results of clashes between the police and Algerians, according to *Le Monde*, Jan. 24–25, 1960, p. 5. Courrière says that from August 21 to September 28, 1958, 242 acts of personal aggression led to 82 deaths, of which 22 were those of metropolitan Frenchmen, and 188 wounded (Yves Courrière, *La guerre d'Algérie*, vol. 3, p. 407).

27. See "Leur Dernière Carte," *El Moudjahid*, no. 12 (Nov. 15, 1957): 9.

28. For further details on the relationship between the FLN and Algerian Jews, see Alistair Horne, *A Savage War of Peace: Algeria 1954–1962* (London: Macmillan, 1977), pp. 58–59, 410–11, and 532–33.

29. *The Freedom Fighter*, Special Issue, 1957, p. 26.

CHAPTER VII

1. Andrew J. R. Mack, "Why Big Nations Lose Small Wars: The Politics of Asymmetrical Conflict," *World Politics* 27, no. 2 (Jan. 1975): 175–200.

2. See Lucien W. Pye, "The Roots of Insurgency and the Commencement of Rebellions," in *Internal War*, ed. Harry Eckstein (New York: Free Press, 1964), pp. 157–79.

3. Ibid., p. 168.

4. Alf Andrew Heggoy, *Insurgency and Counterinsurgency in Algeria* (Bloomington: Indiana University Press, 1972), p. 265.

5. Pye, "The Roots of Insurgency," p. 169.

6. Ibid., p. 170.

7. Ibid., pp. 170–71.

8. David Galula, *Counterinsurgency Warfare* (New York: Praeger, 1964), p. 11.

9. Ibid. Unfortunately the author does not expand on this argument.

10. The respective prime ministers were Pierre Mendès-France, Edgar Faure, Guy Mollet, Maurice Bourgès-Maunoury, Felix Gaillard, and Pierre Pflimlin. De Gaulle was legally the last prime minister of the Fourth Republic, but he governed with special powers.

11. Philip M. Williams, *Crisis and Compromise: Politics in the Fourth Republic* (London: Longmans, 1964), p. 52.

12. See *L'Année Politique*, 1957, pp. 211–12.

13. Yves Courrière, "John Kennedy et Chanderli," *Historia Magazine*, no. 228 (n.d.): 1970–71.

14. See particularly Peter Paret, *French Revolutionary Warfare from Indochina to Algeria* (London: Pall Mall Press, 1964).

15. John Steward Ambler, *The French Army in Politics, 1945–1962* (Columbus: Ohio State University Press, 1966), p. 318.

16. Colonel Broizat's testimony during the trials resulting from the 1960 revolt in Algiers, recorded in *Un procès*, ed. Alain de Sérigny (Paris: La Table Ronde, 1961), pp. 37–38 and quoted in Ambler, *The French Army in Politics*, p. 313.

17. Cf. Paret, *French Revolutionary Warfare*, p. 21; and George A. Kelly, *Lost Soldiers: The French Army and Empire in Crisis, 1947–1962* (Cambridge: The M.I.T. Press, 1965), pp. 107–25.

18. Paret, *French Revolutionary Warfare*, p. 22.

19. *Lost Soldiers*, pp. 116–18. His account refers to Charles Lacheroy, "Scenario-type de guerre révolutionnaire," *Revue des forces terrestres* (Oct. 1956): 25–29; cf. Lucien Poirier, "Un instrument de guerre révolutionnaire: Le FLN," *Revue militaire d'information*, no. 289 (Dec. 1957): 23; and Ximenes (pseud.), "Essai sur la guerre révolutionnaire," *Revue militaire d'information*, no. 281 (Feb.–Mar. 1957): 12–13.

20. "Algérie," *Revue militaire d'information*, Special Issue, No. 269 (Mar. 1956): 4–5.

21. Poirier, "Un instrument," p. 11.

22. Ibid., p. 13.

23. Capitaine Amphioxus (pseud.), "La guerre en Algérie: Regards de l'autre côté," *Revue de défense nationale* 28 (Jan. 1959): 87.

24. Roger Trinquier, *Modern Warfare: A French View of Counterinsurgency* (New York: Praeger, 1964), p. 8; see also p. 52.

25. Roger Trinquier, *Guerre Subversion Révolution* (Paris: Robert Laffont, 1968), pp. 38–39.

26. Ibid., pp. 140–43.

27. Kelly, *Lost Soldiers*, p. 151.

28. See the critique of *quadrillage* in Paret, *French Revolutionary Warfare*, pp. 35–37.

29. Cf. Pierre Boudot, *L'Algérie mal enchaînée* (Paris: Gallimard, 1961), especially pp. 35, 150, and 195–96.

30. Mouloud Feraoun, *Journal 1955–1962* (Paris: Seuil, 1962), pp. 150–51. An *amin* is a Muslim religious official.

31. Paret, *French Revolutionary Warfare*, pp. 45–46.

32. Cf. Kelly, *Lost Soldiers*, pp. 188–89; and Paret, *French Revolutionary Warfare*, pp. 43–45. Pierre Bourdieu gives the total of three million displaced in *The Algerians* (Boston: Beacon Press, 1962) p. 163. A French commander's account of regroupment—remarkable for its disregard for the hardships imposed on the Muslim people—is General Desjours, "Nous avons pacifié Blida," *Historia Magazine*, no. 228 (n.d.): 1064–67.

33. Bourdieu, *The Algerians*, pp. 163, 164, and 175.

34. Ibid., p. 180.

35. Paret, *French Revolutionary Warfare*, p. 45.

36. Ibid., p. 51.

37. See Jacques Duquesne, *L'Algérie ou la guerre des mythes* (Bruges: Desclée de Brouwer, 1958), p. 103.

38. Ambler, *The French Army in Politics*, p. 318.

39. Roger Trinquier, *Guerre Subversion Révolution*, p. 70.

40. Ibid., pp. 155–56.

41. Louis Delarue, *Avec les paras du 1er R.E.P. et du 2e R.P./Ma.* (Paris: Nouvelles éditions latines, 1961)., pp. 49–50.

42. Boudot, *L'Algérie mal enchaînée*, pp. 80–81.

43. Edward Behr, *The Algerian Problem* (London: Hodder and Stoughton, 1961), p. 117.

44. Germaine Tillion, *Les ennemis complémentaires* (Paris: Minuit, 1960), p. 26.

45. Jacques Massu, *La vraie bataille d'Alger* (Paris: Plon, 1971).

46. Ibid., p. 170.

47. Ibid., p. 166.

48. Jules Roy, *J'accuse le général Massu* (Paris: Seuil, 1972). See also his *La guerre d'Algérie* (Paris: Julliard, 1960).

49. Pierre Vidal-Naquet, *La torture dans la république* (Paris: Minuit, 1972). The English translation is *Torture: Cancer of Democracy* (Harmondsworth: Penquin Books Ltd., 1963).

50. Ibid., p. 94 and pp. 109–22.

51. Jacques Pâris de Bollardière, *Bataille d'Alger, bataille de l'homme* (Paris: Desclée de Brouwer, 1972).

52. Ibid., p. 146.

53. Ibid., p. 84.

54. Ibid., pp. 85–87 and 91–94. Cf. Jean-Jacques Servan-Schreiber, *Lieutenant en Algérie* (Paris: Julliard, 1957), for a fictionalized but accurate account of Bollardière's activities.

55. Bollardière, *Bataille d'Alger*, pp. 146–49.

56. Mohamed Lebjaoui, *Bataille d'Alger ou bataille d'Algérie?* (Paris, Gallimard, 1972), p. 10.

57. Ibid., p. 11.

58. Ibid., p. 12.

59. Martin Harrison, "Government and Press in France during the Algerian War," *American Political Science Review* 58, no. 2 (June 1964): 281. Vidal-Naquet, on the other hand, believed that domestic censorship during the war had been effective as a preventive measure because the threat of seizure and subsequent financial loss had been sufficient to cause self-censorship among the press (*La torture dans la république*, p. 163).

60. Duquesne, *L'Algérie ou la guerre des mythes*, pp. 48–49.

CHAPTER VIII

1. The case of Amirouche's leadership of the Kabylia wilaya may be considered an exception to this observation, since the rationality of his actions is questionable.

2. See Chapter 3 of Albert Camus, *L'homme révolté* (in *Essais*, Bibliotheque

de la Pleiade; Paris: Gallimard, 1965) in which he contrasts the two generations of Russian revolutionaries.

3. See the excellent article by Edward Weisband and Damir Roguly, "Palestinian Terrorism: Violence, Verbal Strategy, and Legitimacy," in *Terrorism: National, Regional, and Global Perspectives,* ed. Yonah Alexander (New York: Praeger, 1976), pp. 258–319.

4. See Weisband and Roguly, "Palestinian Terrorism."

5. See J. Bowyer Bell, *On Revolt* (Cambridge: Harvard University Press, 1976), pp. 15–16.

6. For a concise analysis of these factors, see John Dunn, *Modern Revolutions: An Introduction to the Analysis of a Political Phenomenon* (Cambridge: Cambridge University Press, 1972), chap. 6.

Note on Sources

This bibliographical note refers only to the sources that were most relevant to the study of FLN terrorism. Books on the subject of the Algerian war number in the hundreds, so only a small selection will be mentioned here. The literature on terrorism, insurgent warfare, revolution, and the psychology of violence is constantly augmented by new works; this note is meant only as a guide to further study, not as a definitive listing. Many of the books cited here contain specialized bibliographies.

THE ALGERIAN WAR

The four-volume history, *La guerre d'Algérie*, by French journalist Yves Courrière, is indispensable. The series includes *Les fils de la Toussaint, Le temps des léopards, L'heure des colonels,* and *Les feux du désespoir (La fin d'un empire)* (Paris: Fayard, 1968, 1969, 1970, and 1971). In English the most comprehensive account is Alistair Horne, *A Savage War of Peace: Algeria 1954–1962* (London: Macmillan, 1977). Two other works by American journalists appeared before the end of the war but are still valuable: Edward Behr, *The Algerian Problem* (London: Hodder and Stoughton, 1961) and Michael K. Clark, *Algeria in Turmoil* (New York: Grosset and Dunlap, 1960). Also worth mentioning is David C. Gordon, *The Passing of French Algeria* (New York: Oxford University Press, 1963). Brief analyses of the Algerian revolution are included in Eric R. Wolf, *Peasant Wars of the Twentieth Century* (New York: Harper & Row, 1969), and in John Dunn, *Modern Revolutions: An Introduction to the Analysis of a Political Phenomenon* (Cambridge: Cambridge University Press, 1972). Analysis of the social and political background to the war is given in Charles-André Julien, *L'Afrique du Nord en marche: Nationalismes musulmans et souveraineté française,* 3rd ed. (Paris: Julliard, 1972), and in Pierre Bourdieu, *Sociologie de l'Algérie,* 3rd ed. (Paris: Presses universitaires de France, 1970; an earlier edition has been translated with additional material as *The Algerians,* Boston: Beacon Press, 1962). For the French political scene during the crucial period 1954–1958, see Philip M. Williams, *Crisis and Compromise: Politics in the Fourth Republic* (London: Longmans, 1964).

Other secondary sources deal specifically with the role of the FLN. FLN and OAS terrorism are discussed in French journalist Roland Gaucher's *Les terroristes* (Paris: Albin-Michel, 1965; an English translation, *The Terrorists: From Tsarist Russia to the OAS,* was published in London by Secker and Warburg in 1968, but as a result of a successful libel suit against the publisher the edition was withdrawn). Two descriptive accounts in French can be recommended: Jacques C. Duchemin, *Histoire du F.L.N.* (Paris: La Table Ronde, 1962), and Charles-Henri Favrod (a Swiss journalist), *Le FLN et l'Algérie* (Paris: Plon, 1962). For a more analytical perspective, see William Quandt, *Revolution and Political Leadership: Algeria, 1954–1968* (Cambridge: The M.I.T. Press, 1969), and Alf Andrew Heggoy, *Insurgency and Counterinsurgency in Algeria* (Bloomington: Indiana University Press, 1972).

A number of works concentrate on the role of the French army in the post-war era, including Algeria. The most significant is Peter Paret, *French Revolutionary Warfare from Indochina to Algeria* (London: Pall Mall Press, 1964). Also noteworthy are John Steward Ambler, *The French Army in Politics, 1945–1962* (Columbus: Ohio State University Press, 1966); Michel Déon, *L'armée d'Algérie et la pacification* (Paris: Plon, 1959); Raoul Girardet, *La crise militaire française, 1945–1962* (Paris: Armand Colin, 1964); Paul Marie de la Gorce, *La République et son armée* (Paris: Fayard, 1963; translated as *The French Army: A Military-Political History*, New York: G. Braziller, 1963); and George A. Kelly, *Lost Soldiers: The French Army and Empire in Crisis, 1947–1962* (Cambridge: The M.I.T. Press, 1965). Although they nominally deal with broader subjects, Gabriel Bonnet, *Les guerres insurrectionnelles et révolutionnaires* (Paris: Payot, 1958), and Claude Delmas, *La guerre révolutionnaire* (Paris: Presses universitaires de France, 1959), also discuss the French army.

Robert Buchard, *Organisation armée secrète* (Paris: Albin Michel, 1963), and the *Histoire de l'organisation de l'Armée Secrète* (Paris: Julliard, 1964) by Morland, Barangé, and Martinez (pseudonyms of police officers) are detailed descriptions of the OAS. In English, there is Paul Henissart, *Wolves in the City* (London: Rupert Hart-Davis, 1971). Fernand Carréras, *L'accord F.L.N.-O.A.S., des négotiations secrètes au cessez-le-feu* (Paris: R. Laffont, 1967), is an account of a peculiar chapter in the history of both organizations.

The production of memoirs reflecting wartime experiences has been prolific from the French side. The French military is represented by a variety of viewpoints, including those of Jacques Massu in *La vraie Bataille d'Alger* (Paris: Plon, 1971); Jacques Pâris de Bollardière in *Bataille d'Alger, bataille de l'homme* (Paris: Desclée de Brouwer, 1972); Jean-Jacques Servan-Schreiber in *Lieutenant en Algérie* (Paris: Julliard, 1957; an English translation was published in London by Hutchinson in 1958); Yves Godard in *Les paras dans la ville* (Paris: Fayard, 1972); Pierre Leulliette in *Saint Michel et le dragon: Souvenirs d'un parachutiste* (Paris: Minuit, 1961; or *Saint Michael and the Dragon: A Paratrooper in the Algerian War*, London: Heinemann, 1964); Louis Delarue (a French chaplain) in *Avec les paras du 1er R.E.P. et du 2e R.P./Ma.* (Paris: Nouvelles éditions latines, 1961); Paul Mus in *Guerre sans visage: Lettres commentées du sous-lieutenant Emile Mus* (Paris: Seuil, 1961); and Pierre Boudot in *L'Algérie mal enchaînée* (Paris: Gallimard, 1961). Although they are presented primarily as objective studies, Colonel Roger Trinquier's two books, *La guerre moderne* (Paris: La Table Ronde, 1961; translated as *Modern Warfare: A French View of Counterinsurgency*, New York: Praeger, 1964), and *Guerre Subversion Révolution* (Paris: Robert Laffont, 1968), are to a large extent autobiographical.

Other personal recollections, of a political character, include General Charles de Gaulle's *Mémoires d'espoir: Le renouveau 1958–1962* (Paris: Plon, 1970) and Robert Buron, *Carnets politiques de la guerre d'Algérie* (Paris: Plon, 1965). The memoirs of Jacques Soustelle, *Aimée et souffrante Algérie* (Paris: Plon, 1956) and *L'espérance trahie* (Paris: Editions de l'Alma, 1962), concern his experiences as governor-general and as a member of the de Gaulle government. From the European community of Algeria, there are Jacques Chevallier, *Nous, Algériens* (Paris: Calmann-Lévy, 1958), and Albert-Paul Lentin, *Le dernier quart d'heure* (Paris: Julliard, 1963). Albert Camus was also a *pied noir*; see his *Actuelles III: Chroniques Algériennes 1939–1958* (in *Essais*; Bibliothèque de la Pleiade, Paris: Gallimard, 1965). The works on Algeria by the French ethnologist Jean Servier are perceptive: *Dans l'Aurès sur les pas des rebelles* (Paris: France-Empire, 1955); *Adieu djebels* (Paris: France-Empire, 1958); and *Demain en Algérie* (Paris: R. Laffont, 1959). *Les ennemis complémentaires* (Paris: Minuit, 1960), by Germaine Tillion, also a French ethnologist and a liberal member of the Soustelle administration, describes her contacts with the Algiers FLN. The diary of an Algerian novelist expresses the feelings of the moderate intellectuals: Mouloud Feraoun, *Journal, 1955–1962* (Paris: Seuil, 1962). Anne Loesch, a *pied noir* and a member of the OAS, recounted her experiences in *La valise et le cercueil* (Paris: Plon, 1963). *OAS parle* (Paris: Julliard, 1964) is a collection of OAS documents.

Memoirs by members of the FLN are less abundant and much less revealing. Many leaders did not survive the war; of those who did, some remain in Algeria but are politically inactive, some live in exile in Europe, and some (like Belkacem Krim) were murdered. Accounts of their actions by two terrorists are on the whole disappointing: Saadi Yacef, *Souvenirs de la bataille d'Alger* (Paris: Julliard, 1962), and Zohra Drif, *La mort de mes frères* (Paris: Maspéro, 1960). On the bland side are Ferhat Abbas, *Guerre et révolution d'Algérie* (Paris: Julliard, 1962) and Hocine Ait Ahmed, *La guerre et l'après-guerre* (Paris: Minuit, 1964). Mohamed Lebjaoui, *Vérités sur la révolution algérienne* (Paris: Gallimard, 1970), and *Bataille d'Alger ou bataille d'Algérie?* (Paris: Gallimard, 1972), are more forthright on the subject of terrorism. The memoirs of Amar Ouzegane, *Le meilleur combat* (Paris: Julliard, 1962), should also be noted. The works of Frantz Fanon also fall into this category, especially *Les damnés de la terre* (Paris: Maspéro, 1961; translated as *The Wretched of the Earth*, New York: Grove Press, 1968, or London: MacGibbon and Kee, 1965).

The newspapers and periodicals of the time constitute an essential source. The collections of press clippings at the Centre de Documentation of the Fondation National des Sciences Politiques in Paris contain articles from all major newspapers published in French or English, as well as from weekly French periodicals such as *L'Express* and *France-Observateur*. *Le Monde* and *Combat* must be singled out for their objective and thorough reporting of the war. *Esprit* and *La Nef* are also useful sources. From 1971 on, *Historia Magazine* has published a retrospective series of articles on the war, including many personal accounts. The *Revue de défense nationale*, the *Revue militaire d'information*, and the *Revue militaire générale* contain numerous articles on the French military response to terrorism. *L'Année politique* is a detailed official record of events in France and Algeria on a monthly basis. Regular FLN publications in French included *El Moudjahid* and *Résistance Algérienne*.

REVOLUTIONARY TERRORISM

In the past few years academic and governmental interest in terrorism, and consequently the amount of publication on the subject, have grown enormously. However, among general studies, Thomas P. Thornton, "Terror as a Weapon of Political Agitation," in *Internal War: Problems and Approaches,* ed. Harry Eckstein (New York: Free Press, 1964), is still the best starting point for an understanding of the place of terrorism in insurrections. David C. Rapoport, *Assassination and Terrorism* (Toronto: Canadian Broadcasting Corporation, 1971), is a thoughtful essay. Several sociological studies provide theoretical treatments of terrorism: Irving Louis Horowitz, "Political Terrorism and State Power," *Journal of Political and Military Sociology* 1 (Spring 1973): 147–57; Joseph S. Roucek, "Sociological Elements of a Theory of Terror and Violence," *The American Journal of Economics and Sociology* 21 (April 1962): 165–72; and especially Eugene Victor Walter, *Terror and Resistance: A Study of Political Violence* (New York: Oxford University Press, 1969). Another analysis that focuses (like Walter's) on the functions of terrorism for the state, is Alexander Dallin and George W. Breslauer, *Political Terror in Communist Systems* (Stanford: Stanford University Press, 1970).

To put the Algerian case in a wider historical perspective, several comprehensive works that cover a number of examples of terrorism could be consulted. The work by Roland Gaucher, *Les terroristes,* cited in the section on Algeria, is broadly descriptive. In the field of political science, Paul Wilkinson has proposed a typology of terrorist movements in *Political Terrorism* (New York: John Wiley and Sons, 1974). His *Terrorism and the Liberal State* (London: Macmillan, 1977) deals primarily with the modern era. Historian Walter Laqueur, *Terrorism* (London: Weidenfeld and Nicolson, 1977), ranges from nineteenth-century Europe to the 1970s. *Terrorism: National, Regional, and Global Perspectives,* edited by Yonah Alexander (New York: Praeger, 1976), contains articles on different cases of terrorism throughout history. There is also a large body of work focusing on modern international or transnational terrorism, which is beyond the scope of this study. However, readers can be referred to a review article by J. Bowyer Bell, "Trends on Terror: The Analysis of Political Violence," *World Politics* 29 (April 1977): 476–88, and to the *Annotated Bibliography on Transnational and International Terrorism* (Washington: Central Intelligence Agency, 1976).

Literature from the fields of psychology and sociology contributed to the analysis of the motives of terrorists and of the reactions of audiences, although in most cases a long speculative leap had to be made to apply such findings to terrorism in Algeria. Out of the numerous works on violence, aggression, anxiety, stress, and disaster response, the following were helpful: George W. Baker and Dwight W. Chapman, eds., *Man and Society in Disaster* (New York: Basic Books, 1962); Leonard Berkowitz, *Aggression: A Social Psychological Analysis* (New York: McGraw-Hill, 1962); Irving L. Janis, *Air War and Emotional Stress: Psychological Studies of Bombing and Civilian Defense* (New York: McGraw-Hill, 1951); and Maurice R. Stein, Arthur J. Vidich, and David Manning White, eds., *Identity and Anxiety: Survival of the Person in Mass Society* (New York: Free Press, 1960). Leo Lowenthal, "Crisis of the Individual: Terror's Atomization of Man," *Commentary* 1 (January 1946): 1–8, concerns the effects of terror in concentration camps, while the "Document on Terror," in *News from Behind the Iron Curtain* 1 (March 1952): 44–57, purports to be a psychological analysis of the effects of terrorism from the perspective of the totalitarian state. In the field of political science, the adaptation of a psychological approach to the study of violence can be found in the works of Ted Robert Gurr, particularly "Psychological Factors in Civil Violence," *World Politics* 20, no. 2 (January 1968):

245–78, and *Why Men Rebel* (Princeton: Princeton University Press, 1970). An excellent critique of the psychological approach is Peter A. Lupsha, "Explanation of Political Violence: Some Psychological Theories versus Indignation," *Politics and Society* 2 (Fall 1971): 89–104. (The CIA's *Annotated Bibliography* cited above contains sections on "Disaster Response" and "Psychological Approaches to Terrorism," pp. 184–202; Barbara Salert, *Revolutions and Revolutionaries* (New York: Elsevier Scientific Publishing Co., 1976), contains a bibliography (pp. 145–58) on theories and approaches to the study of revolution, including the psychology of violence.)

Theoretical background on the context of revolutionary terrorism came from the vast literature on internal war and revolution. An overview of the field can be found in Harry Eckstein, ed., *Internal War: Problems and Approaches,* (New York: Free Press, 1964). Eckstein's article, "On the Etiology of Internal Wars," *History and Theory* 4 (1965): 133–63, is also valuable. Gurr's *Why Men Rebel* has been cited as an illustration of the psychological approach to revolution; the sociological approach is exemplified by Chalmers Johnson, *Revolutionary Change* (Boston: Little, Brown, and Co., 1966), and the rationalistic approach in Nathan Leites and Charles Wolf, Jr., *Rebellion and Authority: An Analytic Essay on Insurgent Conflicts* (Chicago: Markham Publishing Co., 1970). The book that inspired me to begin this work on Algerian terrorism was Peter Paret and John W. Shy, Jr., *Guerrillas in the 1960s* (New York: Praeger, 1962). Two works already mentioned in reference to the Algerian war are also useful for a comparative perspective: Eric R. Wolf, *Peasant Wars of the Twentieth Century* (New York: Harper & Row, 1969), and John Dunn, *Modern Revolutions: An Introduction to the Analysis of a Political Phenomenon* (Cambridge: Cambridge University Press, 1972). For an instructive contrast, J. Bowyer Bell, *On Revolt* (Cambridge: Harvard University Press, 1976), deals with strategies of rebellion against the British empire.

Finally, two studies were important in the development of the approach used here to analyze FLN terrorism: Arend Lijphart, "Comparative Politics and the Comparative Method," *American Political Science Review* 65 (September 1971): 682–93, and Giovanni Sartori, "Concept Misformation in Comparative Politics," *American Political Science Review* 64 (December 1970): 1033–53.

Index